The Wonder of
GUADALUPE

By the same author:

Books:

Voice of the Saints:
Burns and Oates Golden
Library Series, 1965

Heart of the Saints:
T. Shand Publications, 1975

Alexandrina: The Agony and the Glory:
Veritas Publications, Dublin, 1979

Fatima, the Great Sign:
Augustine Publishing Co., 1980
Tan Book and Publishers, USA, 1981

Pamphlets:

Addict for Christ:
The Story of Venerable Matt Talbot,
C.T.S., 1976

Have You Forgotten Fatima?
C.T.S., 1977

Saint of the Mass:
The Story of St. Charbel Makhlouf,
C.T.S., 1977

The Miracle of Alexandrina:
A.M.I. Publications, USA, 1979

A Very Ordinary Girl:
The Story of Venerable Margaret Sinclair,
C.T.S., 1979

When Millions Saw Mary:
Augustine Publishing Co., 1980

The Wonder of
GUADALUPE

**The Origin and Cult of the Miraculous Image
of the Blessed Virgin in Mexico**

By Francis Johnston

*How beautiful art thou! Thy eyes are
doves' eyes, besides what is hid within.*
Canticle 4:1

TAN BOOKS AND PUBLISHERS, INC.
Rockford, Illinois 61105

The author and the publishers of this book wish to acknowledge the wonderful generosity of Mr. Frank Smoczynski of Addison, Illinois and Dr. Charles Wahlig of Woodside, New York for providing most of the pictures which appear in this book, as well as for their helpful suggestions and advice.

Those who wish to promote devotion to
Our Lady of Guadalupe should write to

> Queen of the Americas Guild
> c/o Father Christopher, O.F.M.
> Capuchin College
> 4121 Harewood Road, N.E.
> Washington, D.C. 20017

Published by TAN Books and Publishers, Inc., in conjunction with Augustine Publishing Company, Chulmleigh, Devon, England.

Library of Congress Catalog Card No. 81-53041

ISBN: 0-89555-168-3

Printed and bound in the United States of America.

TAN BOOKS AND PUBLISHERS, INC.
P. O. Box 424
Rockford, Illinois 61105

1981

CONTENTS

DEDICATION

To my little son,
Anthony

ACKNOWLEDGEMENTS

THE author wishes to express his grateful thanks to the Franciscan Marytown Press for permission to quote from *A Handbook on Guadalupe,* copyrighted 1974; to Dr. C. Wahlig, O.D., for permission to quote from his book *Juan Diego,* copyrighted in 1972 by the author, and to Professor Philip Callahan of the University of Florida, for his kind permission to use brief excerpts from his report on the infra-red radiation investigation of the sacred image in May 1979.

Thanks are also due to Brother Bruno Bonnet-Eymard of Maison Saint Joseph, Saint Parres Les Vaudes, France, for permission to quote from his excellent article entitled "Our Lady and her wonderful image in the light of science and history", which appeared in *The Catholic Counter-Reformation in the XXth Century,* October 1980, No. 127. A word of special thanks is due to my sister, Miss Mary Johnston, B.A., for her excellent map, to Mr. Manuel Perez of De Guadalupe, Los Angeles for his invaluable assistance and to Mr. Peter Croshaw of Crewe, England, for further help in research.

Finally, this book is not intended to be an exhaustive treatise on the subject of Guadalupe, but simply an introduction to enable the reader to become acquainted with the story. While the author has made every effort to achieve the highest accuracy, he would be very grateful to be advised of any omission of importance, or error of fact or interpretation, which may have crept into the work.

AUTHOR'S PREFACE

IT remains one of the great paradoxes of our age that while belief in the existence of God appears to be in general decline, perhaps never before in history has there been so much concrete, scientifically demonstrated evidence confirming His reality. The very technology that is invoked to deny the existence of a Supreme Being has also served to confirm His actuality, in the light of investigations and observations conducted under the most rigorous conditions that modern science can impose. To instance but a few recent examples: the medically confirmed, instantaneous cures of terminal illnesses, contrary to all known laws of science, which occur at Lourdes, Fatima, Banneux and other shrines; the incorrupt body of St. Charbel Makhlouf, the great saint of the Mass, still perspiring blood and water 83 years after his death and officially confirmed by medical science; the stupendous Eucharistic miracle at Lanciano, which leading scientists confirmed in 1971 after an exhaustive investigation; and the 13½ years long fast of the Servant of God Alexandrina da Costa (1942-1955), in which the highest medical authorities certified her subsistence on the Eucharist alone as "scientifically inexplicable".[1]

This book recounts another such prodigy – the sacred image of the Virgin Mary at Guadalupe, Mexico City, the supernatural origin of which was scientifically demonstrated in the 1960s. A thoroughly up-to-date account of the wondrous story in the light of history and modern science is recorded here since relatively little is known of the startling discoveries of recent years concerning the sacred image. For background material, I have relied rather heavily on Fr. Lee's comprehensive and excellent book on the subject, published in 1896, with its numerous references to centuries' old Spanish volumes, which I have footnoted in this work for easy source checking. I also had recourse to the majority of the books listed in the bibliography. To bring the work into the perspective of the 1980s, I drew from a mass of new material, including the recent experiments concerning the eye images in the sacred portrait undertaken by Dr. C. Wahlig, O.D., of New York, one of the greatest living authorities on Guadalupe, the 1979 infra-red radiation investigation of the sublime picture by Professor Philip Callahan of the University of Florida and Professor Jody Smith of Pensacola, Florida, and in particular, from the writings of Brother Bruno Bonnet-Eymard, a leading French authority on Guadalupe who, in October 1980, brilliantly refuted the objections to Guadalupe by certain French agnostic intellectuals.

In recording the dialogue of the Great Event of 1531, I have attempted to follow the story of the apparitions as faithfully as possible, but in certain passages I have excercised an author's right of creative freedom by outlining the likely interior reflections of Juan Diego and Bishop Zumárraga, to strike the spark of life from these historically-distant characters. In several instances I have also amended the original translation of the story by Don Valeriano to a more meaningful and modern rendition.

A further important reason for writing this book is the existence of a widely-held misconception that the cult of Our Lady of Guadalupe, or more precisely, Our Lady of the Americas, is an exclusively New World concern since she appeared in the geographical centre of the Americas in 1531 at a time when these vast regions were beginning to be colonised, and proclaimed herself as "your merciful Mother, the Mother of all who live united in this land." But this is to overlook the fact that she also announced herself as the merciful Mother of "all mankind, of all those who love me, of those who cry to me, of those who have confidence in me . . ."

It is my prayerful hope that this book will help to rectify this unfortunate neglect and draw ever greater numbers of new devotees to her waiting arms – the same arms that once enfolded Christ and that reached down to us from the skies of Fatima in 1917, offering to save us from catastrophe, if we but clasp them with filial love and trust and accept her message of prayer and penitence. This book, written partly during a time of considerable personal trial, is a tribute to the sustaining power of those motherly arms for which I can never adequately express my gratitude. The book should also help to convince the reader that in the sacred image of Our Lady in Mexico City, we have the only true portrait of the Mother of God in existence – the counterpart, if I may express it thus, of the Holy Shroud of Turin.

Francis Johnston,
12 January 1981

---

1. See my recent publications on these subjects: *Fatima, the Great Sign,* Augustine Publishing Co., Devon, England, 1980 and Tan, U.S.A., 1981; *Alexandrina: the Agony of the Glory,* Veritas Publications, Dublin, 1979; and *St. Charbel Makhlouf,* Catholic Truth Society, London, 1977.

I

THE CONQUEST OF MEXICO

THE story of Guadalupe really begins with the arrival of the Spanish forces in Mexico in 1519 under their brilliant commander, Captain Hernando Cortes. As the soldiers penetrated the vast hinterland, across the sandy deserts and expansive green plains, broken by rugged mountains and deep gorges flashing with rivers, they were astonished at the relatively high level of culture attained by the Aztec civilisation they encountered. In many respects, the standards of the Aztecs approached those of Spain itself.

The country of some ten million inhabitants was divided into thirty-eight provinces populated by various tribes which had been subjugated and incorporated into the Aztec Empire. Each province was ruled by a governor, and these dignatories, together with the chief nobles and under the ruling authority of the Emperor in Tenochtitlan (which became Mexico City after the Spanish conquest), controlled the army, levied taxes and directed the interchange of trade and commence. There were accomplished mathematicians, astronomers, architects, physicians, philosophers, craftsmen and artists, while the judicial system bore a striking resemblance to the pattern existing in many European countries. Education began at a very early age, but reading and writing were limited to a pictograph system which was similar to the ancient Egyptian hieroglyphics.

Despite these impressive achievements, the Aztecs were surprisingly backward in some fields of knowledge. They were ignorant of the physical laws that had been demonstrated by the Greeks some 2,000 years earlier. Their mathematicians had no knowledge of experimental science. Nor were they familiar with the wheel, animal traction, or the vaulted arch.

The Aztec towns were usually built around a stone pyramid-shaped temple where they held their religious ceremonies. Nearby would be a large plaza for communal gatherings and a market-place, invariably ringed by prominent stone dwelling-houses belonging to the upper classes, with spacious rooms and interior patios. In some towns, the Spaniards found that their buildings had been erected on raised wooden platforms as a protection against floods. The outskirts were inhabited mostly by the lower classes and consisted of thatch-roofed, windowless houses with walls of wattles smeared with mud. There were several heavily populated cities in the country at the time; Tenochtitlan alone counted 300,000 inhabitants.

Like many contemporary nations in Europe and Asia, the Aztecs had developed a rigid caste system. The highest level consisted of the Emperor, the chief nobles, the chief priests and the judges. Next came the nobles of lower rank who served as administrators. Below them were the *freemen,* the approximate equivalent of our present-day middle class, who constituted the greater number of the population. Under these came the unskilled labourers and the very poor, while at the bottom rung of the social ladder were the slaves.

Agriculture was the leading industry of the country and corn was the chief crop, while others of lesser importance included beans, tomatoes and various fruits in addition to cotton and tobacco. The maguey cactus plant was particularly valued since many useful products could be derived from it. The sap could be fermented and used as a kind of beer, the thorns converted to needles, while its fibre could be twisted into string and rope or woven into material suitable for clothing. Because of their basic importance to the Aztec economy, both corn and the maguey plant were worshipped as goddesses.

This seemingly advanced standard of civilisation was tragically blighted by a religion which sank to some of the worst excesses of superstition. It is difficult for the modern mind to fully comprehend its horror, despite our familiarity with such barbarous modern atrocities as the concentration camp and the practice of 'total war'. The Aztec rituals sprang from a compulsive instinct to attract those natural forces which were beneficial to humans, and to repel those that were malign. Most of these forces, such as the sun, rain, wind, fire and so on, were personalised as gods and goddesses, and idols of these deities were worshipped in the massive pyramidal temples.

The Aztecs felt themselves under a compelling obligation to offer human sacrifices to these gods, either in atonement for some physical calamity, such as a pestilence or earthquake, or to forestall an expected misfortune. For instance, since the Aztecs regarded themselves as the 'people of the sun', they felt driven to supply this divinity with a regular 'nourishment' of human blood, for fear that he might no longer appear on the eastern horizon.

The victims of these sacrifices were most frequently slaves or prisoners of war, and the method of immolation was frightful in the extreme. Tearing out the hearts of living victims by black-robed, long-haired, chanting priests was a relatively merciful death compared to being flayed or eaten alive, and even worse horrors that do not easily lend themselves to words. The killings were on a considerable scale, and occasionally reached thousands in a single day as failure to influence the gods generated a frenzy of slaughter. The bloody hecatomb was actually a horrific inversion of the Christian sacrifice, in which the blood shed by the hapless victims was held to redeem the life of a god, and the continuous application of this human sacrifice was regarded as a solemn duty for the welfare of the people.

The sacrifices were carried out in the great stone temples of each town or city. The mightiest god was Quetzelcoatl, the feathered or stone serpent, to whom many thousands were sacrificed alive each year. Curiously, the name also applied to a great prophet who had reputedly appeared in the dim past and preached a semblance of Christianity which gradually became intermingled with the tenets of paganism. It was widely believed that he would one day return and redeem Aztec society. Another leading deity worth mentioning was the god of war and of the sun, Huitzilopochtli. A frightful temple had been erected in his honour at the town of Tlaltelolco, close to Tenochtitlan, and which the Spaniards found to be a veritable charnel-house. At the inauguration of this temple in 1487, some 20,000 warriors were sacrificed on its altars at the command of the Aztec Emperor, Auitzotl, to appease this monstrous divinity.[1] Perhaps it is significant that the site of this edifice was to play an important role when the healing hand of Christianity began to spread over the land.

In view of what was to come, it is worth mentioning here the great Mother God, Tonantzin, whose temple had once stood on the summit of a small hill named Tepeyac, about six miles to the north of Tenochtitlan. A statue of this grim goddess in the Anthropological Museum in Mexico City today vividly conveys the truly chilling nature of the Aztec mentality. Her head is a combination of loathsome snakes' heads and her garment a mass of writhing serpents. Like the idols of other divinities in the same museum, Tonantzin projects a visage of fathomless grief from her sightless eyes, as if in perpetual mourning over the self-slaughter of her children. Even the nearby idol of the god of joy, Xochipilli, wears a countenance of extreme desolation. Not without reason did the Spanish missionaries, who arrived on the heels of the conquerors, regard this terrible creed as an indication of satanic infestation.

At the time of the Spanish invasion the Emperor of Mexico was the great Montezuma II, who had ascended the throne in 1503. He was a highly superstitious, philosophical man, inclined to witchcraft, and with a vicious streak of tyranny. His harsh rule was bitterly resented by the outlying subject tribes of the Empire and rebellions were frequent. Montezuma's sinister nature, however, also harboured a deep respect for omens and portents, and these seemed to multiply as reports of strange ships being sighted far out to sea reached his attentive ears. Gloomily, he listened to his soothsayers predicting the eventual overthrow of this kingdom by white men from across the ocean.

In 1509 his sister, Princess Papantzin, had an extraordinary dream which seems to have had a decisive influence on the fatalistic Emperor. In that year, she fell seriously ill and lapsed into a coma. Believing her to be dead the Mexicans laid her in a tomb, but hardly had they done so when they were startled to hear her crying out to be released from the coffin. Upon recovering, she related the substance of a profound dream she had just experienced. It seemed that a luminous being had led her to the shore of the boundless ocean and that as she gazed out to sea, a number of large ships materialised with black crosses on their sails which corresponded to the black cross on her guide's forehead. The princess was informed that the vessels were bringing men from a distant land who would conquer the country and bring the Aztecs a knowledge of the true God. The brooding Montezuma read the doom of his Empire in this dream and the fate of Mexico was possibly all but sealed years before the first brightly armoured Spanish soldiers waded ashore from their anchored galleons.

The Mexicans were overawed by the thundering canons and muskets and the superb battle tactics of the advancing Spaniards. Their cavalry seemed invincible to a race that had never set eyes on a horse. To ensure that the white soldiers were indeed the ones seen in his sister's dream, Montezuma had one of the Spanish helmets brought to him, and saw for himself the fateful black cross emblazoned on the front. He consulted with his nobles, and after an indecisive meeting decided to try and buy Cortes off with lavish gifts. The latter's forces had meanwhile been encountering a growing number of regional tribes who detested the iron rule of the Aztecs and yearned to overthrow them. Quickly sizing up the situation, Cortes promised to help them provided they would join forces with him. Soon a growing army of Spaniards and Mexicans were battling their way across the rugged country towards Tenochtitlan. After each victory, their enemies were persuaded to join forces with them in their march on the Aztec capital.

Seeing the balance of fate relentlessly tilting against him, Montezuma felt he had no choice but to await the arrival of Cortes and negotiate a settlement. The Spaniards and their Indian allies advanced cautiously on the city, grimly aware of Montezuma's reputation for treachery, and Cortes kept a wary eye on his new allies as well, for he could not yet be entirely certain of their loyalty.

At that time, Tenochtitlan was surrounded by large lakes and approached by three causeways. One of the Spaniards, Diaz del Castillo, has left us a graphic account of the invaders' first view of Montezuma's fabled capital. "Gazing on such wonderful sights, we did not know whether that which appeared before us was real, for on one side in the land there were great cities and in the lake many more, and the lake itself was crowded with canoes, and on the causeway were many bridges at intervals, and in front of us stood the great city of Mexico and we Spaniards . . . did not number 400 soldiers." [2]

The edges of the island city were fringed with verdure and crowded with white houses and their patio gardens. The metropolis itself was threaded with canals crossed by bridges, somewhat like Venice today, while streets and open squares were few in number. Here and there, great temples thrust skywards like truncated pyramids, and gilded palaces and stately public buildings rose proudly amid teeming markets, zoos, aviaries and gardens of colourful flowers. The Spaniards were full of wonder and respect for the gleaming outward appearances of this pinnacle of Aztec civilisation.

On 8 November 1519, in a ceremony of glittering splendour, Cortes met Montezuma in the presence of his noblemen and grandees. An air of affected amity overlaid their mutual mistrust; Montezuma even arranged for the Spaniards to be quartered in one of the finest palaces of the city. For several days negotiations proceeded and all seemed well on the surface, but Cortes and his men were fully aware of their acute danger. Montezuma had only to give the word and they would have been annihilated in the close confines of the city, where there was no room to deploy against the massed thousands of the Aztec soldiers. Mistrust rapidly developed into animosity and the Spaniards decided that the best form of defence was to seize the initiative. Cortes arrested Montezuma and held him hostage in order to assert Spanish authority and to eliminate the commanding influence of the Emperor. The reaction

MEXICO CITY AND SURROUNDING AREA IN 1531

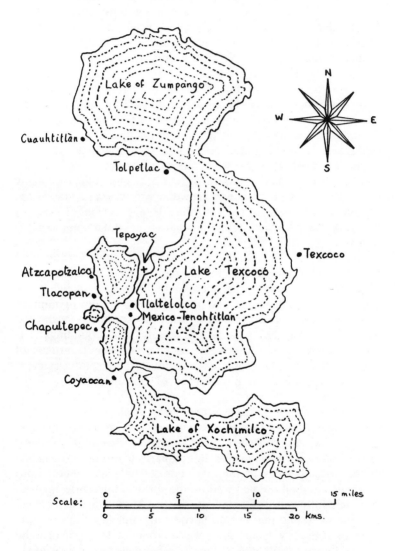

Above: A map showing the Mexico City area as it was in 1531, the year of the apparitions. The lakes have been drained, except Lake Xochimilco. Mexico City now includes all the towns shown here.
Opposite: An artist's conception of Tenochtitlan, as Cortez found it in 1519. It is now part of Mexico City.

Dr. Charles Wahlig

Frank Smoczynski

Upper: A partial view of the Temple of Quetzalcoatl, the Stone Serpent, with the Pyramid of the Sun in the background.
Lower: A reconstructed Aztec wall complete with gargoyles.

Upper left: Statue of Xochipilli, the prince of flowers and god of abundant food, pleasure and love.

Upper right (top): Close-up of the colossal monolithic statue of Coatlicue, a monstrous woman, with jaguar's paws and eagle's claws for feet.

Upper right (bottom): Detail of the famous monolithic Aztec calendar (a huge stone disc) showing Tonatiuh, the sun, whose movement is only maintained by human sacrifices. He puts out his tongue, athirst for blood.

Lower: An artist's depiction of Aztec ritual sacrifice. The victim was laid across a stone and his heart gouged out. The process took only a few seconds. As many as 20,000 victims would be sacrificed at the dedication of a temple.

of the populace was one of tumultuous rage and a frenzied call to arms. An explosion seemed imminent.

At this critical juncture Cortes received word that one of his commanders on the coast had mutinied. Accompanied by a small force of horsemen, he left the city to subdue the uprising. During his absence, the enraged population of Tenochtitlan rose in wrath against the Spaniards. Cortes returned at the height of the savage fighting and after a desperate struggle, during which Montezuma was killed, the Spaniards barely succeeded in extricating themselves from the city. Three-quarters of their soldiers were killed or sacrificed alive in the Aztec temples.

But Cortes was far from finished. He regrouped his depleted forces and, heavily reinforced by his Indian allies, finally succeeded in taking the capital by storm. The Aztec Empire rapidly disintegrated and Mexico was subsequently incorporated under the Spanish crown. Cortes then commenced the monumental task of transforming the centuries-old Aztec culture into a European one.

One of the first acts of the conqueror was to demolish the blood-soaked temples and erect Catholic churches on their sites. The great temple of the feathered serpent-god Huitzilopochtli was replaced by a church named Santiago de Tlaltelolco, which was to play a significant role in the dramatic events to come. Missionaries fanned out across the country, opening churches, schools, and hospitals, but the deep-rooted traditions of paganism proved hard to eradicate and conversions to Christianity were relatively few.

In 1524 Cortes left for Honduras, and during his absence his successor brought false charges against him to the Spanish Emperor, Charles V. A commissioner was sent across the Atlantic to investigate and when Cortes returned from Honduras, he was glad to relinquish control of the still troublesome country to the representative of Charles V. However, the emissary found it virtually impossible to handle the volatile situation, and in 1528 he was replaced by five administrators known as the First Audience. Cortes then returned to Spain to clear his name and receive the honours that were due to a victorious general.

To counterbalance the authority of the First Audience, and to protect the Mexican population from abuse at the hands of their conquerors, Charles V decided to appoint a bishop to the country and to arm him with considerable powers. After careful deliberation, he selected Prior Zumárraga of the Franciscan Monastery of Abrojo in Spain, a priest who had greatly impressed him during a retreat he had made there in the Holy Week of 1527. The Emperor had made him a large gift of money which the Prior accepted under protest and promptly distributed to the poor of the region. In December 1528 Prior Juan Zumárraga was appointed the first Bishop of the New World and sent to Mexico City before his formal consecration.

On arrival in the country, the new Bishop set to work with tireless zeal for the evangelisation and social welfare of Mexico. A man of considerable learning, piety and versatility, whose features in the El Greco painting in the National Archaeological Museum of Mexico City portray a dignified scholar and an ascetic, Zumárraga stove to counter the growing despotism of the First Audience. He brought the first printing press to the continent, imported hitherto unknown fruit trees from Europe to improve the diet of the Mexicans, arranged for the settlement of Spanish agricultural experts to modernise the natives' husbandry and introduced Old World methods of producing linen and silk textiles. The Bishop also established many schools, including the College of the Holy Cross at Tlaltelolco near Mexico City, of which we shall hear more later, and he paved the way for the foundation of the first university in the country – today the largest in the world with some 90,000 students.

Zumárraga was even more zealous for the spiritual welfare of the Mexicans. He prevailed on the Church in Spain to send out many missionaries and fostered the training of native clergy in the seminaries which he founded. But the roots of paganism were deeply implanted in the Aztec soul; the vast majority of Mexicans were loth to abandon the ancestral worship of idols, and baptisms were few and far between. To add to the missionaries' difficulties, the First Audience was dominated by Don Nune de Guzman, who was rapidly acquiring a reputation for cruelty and tyranny in the exercise of the powers entrusted to him by the distant Charles V.

Guzman attempted to justify his harsh rule on the grounds that the Aztecs were soul-less beings akin to the monsters of ancient legends,[3] whom it was a waste of time to evangelise and who could legitimately be exploited. The missionaries, however, insisted that since the Indians were endowed with reason they could become sons of God through Baptism and therefore had every right to be treated with respect.

Zumárraga's persistent representations were of no avail. Goaded by avarice, the rulers tortured and murdered many innocent citizens, and when the Bishop sternly protested, a number of his friars were assaulted by Guzman, who even felt strong enough to threaten Zumárraga himself. The severe persecution to which the Bishop was subjected, as a consequence of his unwearying efforts to uphold the rights of the Indians in the subsequent administration, goes a considerable way towards explaining his relative silence on the dramatic event that was about to take place. "The persecution that the president and his judges carry on against the monks and the clergy," he wrote "is worse than that of Herod and Diocletian."[4]

Finally the Bishop managed to evade Guzman's tight censorship and succeeded in smuggling a message back to Charles V in Spain in a hollowed-out crucifix. The Emperor immediately replaced Guzman and his tyrannical officials with a Second Audience headed by a man of unquestioned integrity, Bishop Don Sebastian Ramirez y Fuenleal. Though the appointments were made in 1530, it took time for the nominees to terminate their affairs in Spain and make the three-month-long voyage across the Atlantic, and they had still not arrived in Mexico by the following year.

Meanwhile, the Aztecs and other tribes of the country had been driven by the cruelty of the First Audience to take up arms against the Spaniards. Zumárraga sensed that a general insurrection was imminent and begged Our Lady to intervene and avert the eruption of a violent explosion which threatened to annihilate the relatively few Spaniards in the country.[5] Secretly he asked the Blessed Virgin to send him some Castilian roses, then unknown in Mexico, as a sign that his desperate prayer had been heard.

In passing, it should be borne in mind that the cruelty of the Spaniards in their dealings with the recently defeated Mexicans was largely confined to the rulers, and that a sizeable proportion of the settlers strove to forge genuine bonds with the natives by means of intermarriage and by attempting to fuse their two cultures and traditions into a new nation. The civil rights of the majority were finally secured by Charles V when he established a Council of the Indies at Seville in 1542 to deal with complaints and violations of justice in the New World. It should also be remembered that much of the vilification of Cortes's work and that of his successors was grossly exaggerated, especially by a certain Bartolomé de las Casas, chaplain to Diego Velasquez, conqueror of Cuba. This man engaged in a bitter personal feud with Cortes and many of his fellow countrymen in Mexico. His wildly distorted charges were seized on by English, French and Dutch Protestants in Europe eager to discredit the work of Catholic missionaries in the New World.

NOTES

1. The site of this temple was discovered on 21 February 1978, a stone's throw from the Cathedral in Mexico City, and is now undergoing extensive excavations.
2. Diaz del Castillo, 1908-16, Vol. 2, Chap. 88.
3. This thinking had been graphically expressed in a number of engravings of the New World dating from the time of the discoveries of Christopher Columbus. But certain high-ranking Spaniards, notably Queen Isabella, insisted that the Indians were true human beings and those brought to Spain as slaves were freed at her command. Intervening in the debate in 1537, Pope Paul III promulgated the brief *Cardinali toletano* and the bull *Sublimis Deus* in which he upheld the humanity of the Indians. Five years later, Charles V promulgated his New Laws of the Indies, in which the Mexicans became free subjects of the Spanish Crown.
4. *Life of Bishop Zumárraga,* by Garcia Icazbalceta: Appendix.
5. Some historians concede that had the insurrection occurred, the Aztecs would certainly have wiped out the Spanish presence in Mexico, thus profoundly transforming the course of history. cf. *Juan Diego,* by Dr. Charles Wahlig, O.D., p.77.

II

THE VISIONS AT TEPEYAC

AMONG the first Mexicans to receive baptism was Princess Papantzin in 1525. When in the same year, a poor peasant and his wife from the village of Cuautitlan, some 15 miles north east of Mexico City were likewise received into the church, he took the name of Juan Diego and his spouse became Maria Lucia.[1] Also among the first Christians was his uncle, Juan Bernardino, who lived at the village of Tolpetlac some six miles to the south of Cuautitlan.

Juan had been born in 1474 just eighteen years before Columbus first sighted San Salvador, and after losing his parents in childhood, Juan was brought up by his uncle. On marrying, he moved to Cuautitlan where he settled with his wife in a little one-roomed mud house thatched with corn stalks. He devoted himself to farming, weaving mats out of reeds cut from the nearby lakes, and making furniture, as well as hiring himself out for whatever work was available in the vicinity. He also owned a house and some land in Tolpetlac. Both his homes were sturdily built and survive to this day in a remarkably good state of preservation.

Juan was rather a small man with a friendly but reserved nature. From the little we know of him, his abiding virtue seems to have been humility. He was quietly unassuming and when walking he was inclined to stoop and shuffle along. Though he belonged to the middle class and must have had a rudimentary education, he was in reality as poor as the lowest class. Life for him was a continual struggle for survival. He found solace however in his new faith, which he practiced with an ardent devotion. It is instructive that he offered himself for instruction and baptism only two years after the first Franciscans had landed in Mexico.

Frequently, Juan and his wife would walk the 15 miles to Tlaltelolco to attend Mass and receive the sacraments and further instruction in the Faith. They would rise long before dawn to begin the 30-mile journey on foot over the hills, for the missionaries had stressed the importance of arriving early for Mass. Like most of their race, Juan and his wife had been accustomed to such long treks since childhood, but with the onset of middle age the broken undulating terrain must have told increasingly on his strength.

On arriving at the new Franciscan Convent in Tlaltelolco, Juan would sit on the hard ground beside his wife, in company with hundreds of other Mexicans, and listen while the friars patiently instructed them in the new Faith. Phrases like *Amar a Dios* (Love God) and *Santa Maria* (Holy Mary) flowed easily from his joyous lips. The contrast between the horrors of paganism and the love, joy and vibrant hope of Christianity could not have been more absolute.

Life for Juan passed on smoothly and uneventfully, until suddenly in 1529 Maria Lucia died. The shock to this simple Mexican peasant was understandably severe. Childless, he found life in the empty house, with its silent loom, the vacant table, and the lonely evenings, almost unbearable. Finally he decided to leave Cuautitlan and live near his aged uncle in Tolpetlac, which had the added advantage of being only nine miles from the church in Tlaltelolco. He had been deeply devoted to his uncle, and since the latter lived alone Juan could now spend much of his time caring for him. In between, he carried on his rustic life, cultivating corn and beans and occasionally hunting for venison.

He continued his regular journeys over the broad hills to Mass, though by 1531, when he had reached the age of 57, he was beginning to tire more easily. The distance was far too long for his aged uncle, and when Juan set off for Tlaltelolco in the chill darkness before dawn he must have felt the loneliness close in, and we can imagine how he sighed for the companionship of his dear wife.

On the morning of Saturday 9 December 1531, which was then the feast of the Immaculate Conception of the Blessed Virgin, Juan rose early and, leaving his house in the cold starlight, began the long walk across the undulating country to assist at the Mass in honour of his Mother and his Queen. There was something special for him about this particular feast. Had not the good friars explained how the Mother of Christ had been born without the stain of original sin, how she had been redeemed in advance in anticipation of the merits of Calvary? And she, the all-pure and shining one, the celestial Queen of Heaven, was his own personal Mother. He felt his melancholy life, his pace quicken as the stars paled above him, and as he hurried along with these thoughts he scarcely paid heed to the bitterly cold wind gusting down from the barren hills and the sharp stones cutting into his leather sandals.

Approaching the shoulder of Tepeyac hill, with its long-forgotten memories of the former pagan temple of Tonantzin, he was startled to hear strains of music in the still morning twilight. He stopped abruptly and listened. Perhaps it was his imagination . . . But no, the music was real and, what was even more astonishing, the strains were beautiful beyond words, like a choir of mellifluous birds, filling the chilly air with ravishing sweetness, intoxicating his senses. Juan gazed up in wonderment at the dark outline of Tepeyac Hill from where the blissful harmony flowed down like liquid silver. To his amazement he saw a glowing white cloud, emblazoned by a brilliant rainbow formed by rays of dazzling light streaming from the cloud. All at once, the thrilling melody ceased without the trace of an echo. Then he heard someone calling to him from the misty summit – a woman's voice, gentle and insistent, that seemed to go straight through him like a golden spear. "Juanito . . . Juan Dieguito," she called affectionately, using the diminutive of his name.[2]

Juan peered up towards the rocky hilltop, feeling himself inwardly drawn to respond to the mysterious summons. Unafraid, he clambered up the boulder-strewn slope and on reaching the 130-foot-high summit, he suddenly found himself face to face with a Lady of overpowering brilliance and beauty. Her garments shone like the sun and the radiance of her person suffused the surrounding rocks, mezquite bushes, prickly pears and other scrubby plants growing nearby, spangling them with a riot of colour, as if they were being viewed through the stained glass windows of some magnificent cathedral. She appeared to be young, perhaps fourteen, and as she beckoned to him to approach, Juan hesitantly took several paces forward and sank to his knees in veneration, dazed by the overwhelming loveliness of the vision.

"Juanito, my son, where are you going?" Her voice was low and gentle, her tone full of esteem.

"Noble Lady," he heard himself murmur, "I am on my way to the church in Tlaltelolco to hear Mass."

The Lady smiled approvingly and said: "Know for certain, dearest of my sons, that I am the perfect and perpetual Virgin Mary, Mother of the True God, through whom everything lives,[3] the Lord of all things, who is Master of Heaven and Earth. I ardently desire a *teocalli* (temple)[4] be built here for me where I will show and offer all my love, my compassion, my help and my protection to the people. I am your merciful Mother, the Mother of all who live united in this land, and of all mankind, of all those who love me, of those who cry to me, of those who have confidence in me. Here I will hear their weeping and their sorrows, and will remedy and alleviate their sufferings, necessities and misfortunes. Therefore, in order to realise my intentions, go to the house of the Bishop of Mexico City and tell him that I sent you and that it is my desire to have a *teocalli* built here. Tell him all that you have seen and heard. Be assured that I shall be very grateful and will reward you for doing diligently what I have asked of you. Now that you have heard my words, my son, go and do everything as best as you can."

Juan bowed very low and said reverently, "My Holy One, my Lady, I will do all you ask of me." He then took leave of her and descending the rocky slope of Tepeyac, set off in rapt wonder towards Mexico City.

The sun had barely risen in the chill blue sky when Juan crossed the main causeway over Lake Texcoco and passed through the northern gate of the city. As he threaded his way through the sleepy town to Bishop Zumárraga's house, he wondered uneasily how he would be received by the prelate, for he was uncomfortably aware of his coarse clothing and lowly status. He doubted if the Bishop would believe his improbable story. Worse, His Excellency's servants might beat him or set their dogs on him for daring to disturb their house at this early hour. His heart flinched at the prospect, but since it was the Queen of Heaven who had entrusted him with this mission, he was determined to see it through.

Slowly and deliberately he knocked on the door of the episcopal residence. It was opened by a servant. Juan asked to be taken to the Bishop. Predictably, the servant was taken aback by his unkempt appearance and eyed him suspiciously. Juan patiently repeated his request. After some hesitation, the servant seemed to change his mind and standing aside, grudgingly ushered him into a patio where he was told to sit down and wait.

An hour dragged by. Juan began to wonder how much longer he would have to sit there in the biting cold air. The keen wind cut into him like a knife – the city is 7,000 feet above sea level – and he drew his cloak or *tilma* closer round his shivering body and rubbed his hands together in an effort to keep warm. Finally an official materialised in the doorway and announced that His Excellency was ready to receive him.

Bishop Zumárraga rose to greet his unusual visitor with his habitual courtesy and kindness and summoned an interpreter, a Spaniard named Juan Gonzalez. The latter was a well educated 31-year-old man who had learnt the Aztec language while travelling round the vast country helping the far-flung mission stations. In consequence, he had been appointed official interpreter to the Bishop and had become a member of the episcopal household.

Kneeling before the prelate and suppressing his nervousness, Juan Diego recounted his extraordinary experience as best he could and repeated the Lady's message exactly as he had heard it. The Bishop puckered his high brow and searched the Mexican's bronzed, weatherbeaten face, trying to determine whether he was speaking the truth. As he listened, he couldn't help being impressed by Juan's evident sincerity and humility. He asked him where he lived and what was his occupation, and then questioned him on the gospels and the practice of his religion. Juan's answers satisfied the Bishop, but as for the story of the Queen of Heaven appearing to him . . . Zumárraga sighed, and hesitated.

The Bishop shook his head slowly. And as Juan stared at him in dismay, the prelate laid his hand gently on his shoulder and said in a mollifying tone, "You must come again, my son, when I can hear you more at my leisure. Meanwhile, I will reflect on what you have told me and I will take careful consideration of the good will and the earnest desire that caused you to come to me." He gave him a sign of dismissal and Juan rose to his feet crestfallen, conscious that he had failed in the Lady's mission. Although he had half expected as much, nevertheless the Bishop's negative decision had given him a shock. The next moment, he found himself being escorted through the spacious building, past occasional knots of officials and servants eyeing him with amused contempt, and so out into the dusty street. True, his Excellency had been kind and condescending, but the animosity of his household had accentuated his bitter disappointment. With a heavy heart he trudged northwards through the city and across the long causeway in the direction of Tepeyac.

As he approached the rocky hill, Juan suddenly felt instinctively certain that the Lady clothed in light would be waiting for him at the summit. He clambered up the stony slope and found her standing there, bathed in the same supernatural radiance that he had seen earlier. He fell to his knees at once, bowing low in veneration. "Noble Lady", he breathed, "I obeyed your orders. I entered into the Bishop's audience chamber, though I had difficulty in doing so. I saw His Excellency as you asked of me. He received me kindly and listened with attention, but when he answered me, it seemed as if he did not believe me." Juan hesitated, biting his lip with disappointment. "He said to me: 'You must come again sometime, my son, when I can hear you more at my leisure. I will reflect on what you have told me and I will take careful consideration of the good will and the earnest desire that caused you to come to me.' I knew by the manner of his response that he thought I was inventing the story of your desire to have a temple built here . . . So I beg you, noble Lady, entrust this message to someone of importance, someone well-known and respected, so that your wish will be accomplished. For I am only a lowly peasant and you, my Lady, have sent me to a place where I have no standing. Forgive me if I have disappointed you for having failed in my mission."

The Virgin smiled tenderly on him and said, "Listen to me, my dearest son, and understand that I have many servants and messengers whom I could charge with the delivery of my message. But it is altogether necessary that you should be the one to undertaken this mission and that it be through your mediation and assistance that my wish should be accomplished. I urge you to go to the Bishop again tomorrow. Tell him in my name and make him fully understand my disposition, that he should undertake the erection of the *teocalli* for which I ask. And repeat to him that it is I in person, the ever Virgin Mary, the Mother of God, who send you."

Gazing on her ineffable countenance, Juan felt a surge of reassurance and replied, "Holy Lady, I will not disappoint you. I will gladly go again at your command, even though once more I may not be believed. Tomorrow towards sunset, I shall return here and give an account of the Bishop's response." With that Juan rose to his feet and giving the radiant Presence a last longing look, bowed very low and took his leave of her.

On arriving home, he cooked his supper and went straight to bed, for he was very tired and there was another long journey ahead of him the next morning, which was Sunday. Some hours later he rose in the darkness and after an uneventful journey, arrived at the church of Santiago in Tlaltelolco for Mass and further instruction in Christian doctrine. It was almost ten o'clock by the time he left the church and set off for nearby Mexico City. As he shuffled along, his mind wrestled with the problem of how to persuade the Bishop's servants to take him to His Excellency so soon again. And how was he to convince the prelate that he was speaking the truth? The thought of failure disconcerted him. Suppose the servants refused to admit him and set their guard dogs on him? They had only to shout an order and he would suffer a severe mauling. Juan murmured a prayer to the Blessed Virgin and set his face resolutely towards the Bishop's house. Surely she would help him maintain his courage and secure him a second audience.

On reaching the Bishop's residence, he was not surprised when he was greeted with ill-concealed exasparation. His Excellency was preoccupied with more important matters, he was brusquely informed, and would be unable to see him. Juan persisted with his request, finally wore down the servants' resistance and was grudgingly admitted to the patio once again, where he was told to wait. From the tone of the servant's voice, he sensed that he might have to suffer another long delay.

The cold wind gusted fitfully through the patio, and he drew his *tilma* closer as he paced up and down, trying to think how he could convince the Bishop that the vision he had seen was genuine. Every now and then an official would brush by, some of them perhaps throwing him a scornful glance in passing. Juan pretended not to notice, but he felt humiliated and unsettled. He was convinced that they regarded him as an ignorant Indian, but there was another agony gnawing at his heart: how was he going to convince them that he spoke the truth?

Finally, after several hours waiting, someone called out his name and he was conducted to the Bishop.

Zumárraga looked up, startled at seeing him back so soon. But he received him with his habitual courtesy, unaware that his visitor had been detained for so long. Juan at once threw himself on his knees before the prelate and repeated the Lady's message with all the fervour at his command. But his own intensity, and the long, chilly wait he had endured, overcame him. The tears started from his eyes, and the words tumbled out passionately as he pleaded with clasped hands for compliance with the Lady's request.

Zumárraga was embarrassed at this strange behaviour. He laid a hand on the Mexican's shoulder and in a kind, paternal tone, urged him to recollect himself and answer his questions. Juan drew a deep breath, and recovered his composure. "Where did you see her?" the Bishop asked. "What was she like?" "How long did she stay?" The Mexican recounted everything that had happened at Tepeyac, and during the searching cross-examination that followed, he never once contradicted the slightest detail of his story.

Zumárraga was impressed, but he was not going to be induced into building a temple at that remote spot simply on the basis of one Indian's unproven testimony. How could he be sure that the man was not suffering from some form of self-delusion? He needed something more convincing, such as a sign from Heaven. On hearing this, Juan felt a surge of hope. "Señor," he asked eagerly, "just what kind of sign do you ask for? I shall go at once and request it of the Lady of Heaven who sent me."

Surprised, perhaps, at this reply, the Bishop hesitated, and then indicated that he would leave it to the supposed vision to supply the sign. And with that, Juan was dismissed.

Immediately he had gone, Zumárraga ordered several trusted aides to follow him and secretly to observe where he went and to whom he spoke. This was done and, maintaining a discreet distance from Juan, they kept him in view through the city gate and along the causeway to Tepeyac. On reaching a ravine by the hill, he suddenly disappeared from their sight. The Bishop's men searched everywhere, clambering over rocks and peering into gullies, but he was nowhere to be seen. Annoyed at all the trouble he had caused, they finally abandoned their search and trudged back to the city, where they told the Bishop that the Mexican was clearly an imposter who had deluded them all, and they suggested that if he had the impudence to show up again he should be punished and taught a lesson. Zumárraga said nothing. He had resolved to withold his judgement pending the outcome of his request for a sign.

While the search for Juan had been going on, he had climbed the rugged slope of Tepeyac and found himself once again in the radiant presence of the Mother of God. The bright aura surrounding her enveloped him like a luminous mist, concealing his whereabouts. He threw himself at her feet and poured out his heart in a flood of sorrow. No one had believed his story. He had done his best, but had failed. Would the Lady please give him a sign to convince the Bishop that he was indeed speaking the truth.

When his auguished voice was finally silent, the Lady smiled tenderly at him in full appreciation of all his efforts. "That is very well, my little son. Return here tomorrow and you will have the sign he has requested. Then he will believe and no longer doubt or suspect you." Her smile grew even more affectionate. "Mark my words well, my little son: I shall richly reward you for all the worry, work and trouble you have undertaken on my behalf. You may go home now. Tomorrow, I shall be waiting here for you."

Juan returned to Tolpetlac full of joy at the Lady's words, feeling a great burden lifted from his shoulders. That evening he went across to see his beloved uncle Juan Bernardino, and was horrified to find him lying seriously ill with *cocolixtle,* a dreaded fever that invariably claimed the lives of its victims. Juan immediately summoned the village physician, who did his best to alleviate the old man's sufferings with herbal remedies, but his condition continued to deteriorate.

All that night and throughout the following day, Juan Diego sat broken-hearted by his uncle's bedside, ministering to his needs and comforting him as best he could. Surely the Lady would understand his predicament and excuse his absence from Tepeyac. Towards sunset, it became clear that his uncle was dying. The stricken man pleaded with his nephew to hurry to Tlaltelolco early next morning to bring a priest to hear his confession and administer the last sacraments. Accordingly, Juan set off about four in the morning, walking as fast as he could, for he knew his uncle might have only a few hours left to live.

Researchers have often wondered why Juan failed to have confidence in the power of the Blessed Virgin at this critical juncture. It seems surprising that, having seen and spoken with her and knowing that she would be waiting for him again, his first thought was not rather to have kept his rendezvous with her and pleaded in person for his uncle's life. The late Helen Behrens, one of the greatest modern authorities on Guadalupe, undertook a searching investigation into this difficulty, interviewing many of the inhabitants of Tolpetlac where a tradition of the events of 1531 has been passed down from generation to generation. She discovered that they maintain a very different version of this episode, according to which, when Juan returned home on the Sunday evening, he found that his uncle was missing. After an anxious search he discovered him lying face down on the edge of a nearby wood, fatally wounded by an arrow. The general insurrection against the Spaniards was imminent and Juan Bernardino, a Christian, had been shot for collaborating with the Spanish missionaries. His nephew carried him back to his house, distracted with grief, unable to comprehend why this awful tragedy should have happened just at the moment of his breath-taking encounter with the Mother of God.

Perhaps the Bishop was right after all. Maybe he was only imagining the visions, or suffering from hallucinations. Doubtless it was in consequence of thoughts such as these revolving in his mind that he decided not to keep his appointment with the Lady the following day. If this was the reason, that would explain his acute embarrassment when he subsequently met her on the Tuesday morning. Helen Behrens also discovered that a stone cross had been erected at the spot where Juan Bernardino was reportedly shot. For several centuries it had disappeared, probably swallowed up in the marshy terrain, but about seventy years ago it was brought to light again at its traditional location, following the convulsions of an earthquake.

The morning of Tuesday, 12 December found Juan Diego hurrying along the path to Tlaltelolco. As he approached Tepeyac Hill, he came to a decision regarding a dilemma that had been troubling him on the way. If he passed the hill on the usual side, the Lady would see him and detain him in order to give him the sign which she had promised him for the Bishop. But Juan had not a moment to lose if he was to fetch a priest before his uncle died. Accordingly, he struck off across the rough, grassy ground and skirted the hill on the east side, where he hoped to slip by unseen.

As he passed the prominence, he was suddenly startled to see her descending from the hill in a blaze of light some distance ahead and approaching at an angle where she would intercept him. Overcome by shame and confusion, and uncertain what to do, he then heard her calling to him in her usual kind, compassionate voice. "What is the matter, my little son?" she said. "Where are you going?"

He approached her in bewilderment and bowing low, heard himself mumbling pleasantries to try to conceal his embarrassment. Then he regained control of himself and in a calmer voice said, "Noble Lady, it will grieve you to hear what I have to say. My uncle, your poor servant, is very sick. He is suffering from the plague and is dying. I am hurrying to the church in Mexico City to call a priest to hear his confession and give him the last rites. When I have done this, I will return here immediately to convey your message." He hesitated and his eyes pleaded with her. "Please forgive me and be patient with me. I am not deceiving you. I promise faithfully to come here tomorrow with all haste."

There was a pause. He could see love and sympathy flowing from the Lady's steadfast gaze, and the tenderness of her gentle response moved him almost to tears. "Listen and let it penetrate your heart, my dear little son," she said consolingly, in words that were to echo down the centuries, moving millions of her children to throw themselves into her comforting arms. "Do not be troubled or weighed down with grief. Do not fear any illness or vexation, anxiety or pain. Am I not here who am your Mother? Are you not under my shadow and protection? Am I am not your fountain of life? Are you not in the folds of my mantle? In the crossing of my arms? Is there anything else you need?" She paused, smiling at him, and then added, "Do not let the illness of your uncle worry you because he is not going to die of his sickness. At this very moment, he is cured."

In these sublime words, uttered to a humble Mexican peasant, Our Lady disclosed to all her suffering children the exquisite tenderness of her Immaculate Heart. Her words are a personal message of deep love and maternal solicitude destined for each one of us, regardless of our creed, our colour, our race or our class. The glorious Mother of God had come to the barren hill of Tepeyac, later to become the site of a vast and world-famous shrine, as the compassionate Mother of all mankind, the Mother of pity and of grace, the Mother of mercy to whom Our Lord in His hour of extreme agony on the cross entrusted us, in order that, as He intercedes with His Heavenly Father for us, she may likewise intercede with her Son on our behalf.[5]

The consolation experienced by Juan Diego on hearing the Mother of God utter such tender words to him may well be imagined. On recovering from his joyous bewilderment, he offered to set out at once for the Bishop's palace with the promised sign. The lady smiled approvingly and told him to climb to the summit of Tepeyac "to the spot where you saw me previously. There you will find many flowers growing. Gather them carefully, assembly them together, and then bring them back and show me what you have."

Juan climbed up the hill with alacrity, and on reaching the crest was amazed to find a brilliant profusion of flowers, including Castilian roses, blooming in the frozen soil. Not only were they in bloom completely out of season, but it would have been quite impossible for any flowers to grow in a terrain so stony that it could only yield thistles, cactus and mezquite bushes. He noticed that the flowers glittered with dewdrops and that their delicious fragrance rose like a breath of Paradise.

Spreading out his *tilma* like an apron, he filled it with the colourful blooms and descended to where the Lady was waiting for him in an oval blaze of light. When he showed her the glowing heap of flowers, she re-arranged them carefully with her own hands, saying as she did so: "My little son, these varied flowers are the sign which you are to take to the Bishop. Tell him in my name that in them he will recognise my will and that he must fulfill it. You will be my ambassador, fully worthy of my confidence. I enjoin you not to unfold your *tilma,* nor to reveal its contents, until you are in his presence. Then tell him everything: explain how I sent you to the top of the hill where you found these flowers growing in profusion, all ready to be gathered. Tell him once again all that you have seen and heard here to induce him to comply with my wishes so that the *teocalli* I asked for may be built here."

Juan nodded his understanding, and holding the fringe of his *tilma* carefully against his chest so as not to crush any of the delicate blooms, he bowed reverently and took his leave, heading for the causeway to Mexico City. His heart beat exultantly as he walked along, for this time the Bishop would have to believe him. Every now and then he stopped to ensure that the precious flowers remained exactly as the Lady had arranged them. Their exquisite fragrance seemed to impel him forward; he so longed for the moment when the Bishop would finally accept his story and order the building of a temple at Tepeyac. Though he knew there might be trouble again with the servants at the gate, this time he felt sure that somehow all the obstacles would be overcome.

No sooner had he arrived at the Bishop's house than the servants rushed out angrily to drive him away. Juan stood his ground, imploring them to take him to the Bishop just once more, insisting that this time His Excellency would certainly believe his story. They refused, pretending not to understand him. Abuse was hurled at him as the metal gates were clanged shut in his face. Juan refused to go away, determined to wait by the gates all day if necessary to wear them out with his persistent pleading.

An hour or so later, one of the officials inside the compound noticed that he was still there, clutching the ends of his *tilma* as if he were concealing something. He asked Juan what he was carrying, but was unable to elicit a satisfactory reply. On hearing this intriguing exchange, several other members of the household materialised, opened the gates, and gathered round the Mexican, demanding that he open up his *tilma*. When he refused, they threatened to use force. Realising that they were in earnest, Juan reluctantly opened the *tilma* a fraction to allow them a brief glimpse of the flowers. They gasped at the sight of the magnificent blooms and were all but overcome by their exquisite fragrance. Avidly, they tried to snatch at them, but as they did so the flowers seemed to melt into the sides of the *tilma* as if they were an embroidery. One of them then dashed off to report this extraordinary event to the Bishop. Zumárraga, once again unaware that Juan had been kept waiting, wondered this time if he had brought the sign which he had requested and ordered Juan to be admitted to his presence at once.

Juan found the Bishop surrounded by a number of imposing-looking personages, including Bishop Don Sebastian Ramirez y Fuenleal, the new governor of Mexico. He bowed low instead of kneeling, for fear of losing his hold on the *tilma,* and recounted what had transpired at Tepeyac, Juan Gonzales again acting as his interpreter. "Your Excellency," Juan said, "I obeyed your instructions. Very early this morning, the celestial Lady told me to come and see you again. I asked for the sign which you requested and which she had promised to give me. She told me to climb to the top of the hill where I had previously seen her, to pick the flowers growing there. I knew quite well that the summit of the hill was no place for flowers to grow, especially at this time of the year, but I did not doubt her word. When I reached the top, I was astonished to find myself surrounded by beautiful flowers, all brilliant with dewdrops. I plucked as many as I could carry and brought them back to her. She arranged them with her own hands and replaced them in my robe in order that I might bring them to you. Here they are. Behold, receive them." With that, Juan released the ends of his *tilma* and the flowers, mingled with Castilian roses, cascaded to the floor in a profusion of colour and perfume.

Zumárraga gazed at them, momentarily speechless. It was the sign he had asked of the Blessed Virgin to show that she had heard his prayer for peace in the country. Full of wonder, he lifted up his eyes to the *tilma* and at that instant there appeared on it a glorious image of the Mother of Christ.

For one electrifying moment, the eyes of every person in that hushed room were rivetted on the glowing image as if they were contemplating an apparition. Then slowly they sank to their knees in awe and veneration. Utterly perplexed, Juan glanced down at the object of their gaze to see what it was that had transfixed them, and was overwhelmed to find himself contemplating an exact replica of the celestial Lady he had seen at Tepeyac.

Juan's eyes shone in stupefaction. So she had come almost in person, it seemed, to confront the Bishop with this further incontestable sign, a wondrous visual representation of her very self, which millions down the centuries were to contemplate with the same awe and veneration that he now saw reflected in the faces of the Bishop and his entourage.

When Zumárraga finally rose to his feet, he embraced Juan and begged his forgiveness for having doubted him. He invited Juan to remain for the night as his honoured guest and promised to accompany him next day to the blessed spot where the Mother of God had asked for a temple to be erected. With the utmost care, the Bishop untied the *tilma* at the back of Juan's neck and reverently conveyed the transfigured garment to his private oratory where he could contemplate it to his heart's content.

News of the prodigy spread like wild fire throughout the city and the following morning the sacred image was borne in triumphant procession to the cathedral, accompanied by joyous multitudes. Towards midday, the Bishop and his retinue accompanied Juan to the site of the apparitions.

After consultation, Zumárraga decided that a small chapel should be built immediately until more elaborate plans for a much larger and really worthy shrine could be drawn up and put in hand. When everything had been settled, Juan asked permission to retire, for he was impatient to return home to his uncle. He did not doubt the Lady's assurance that he had been cured, but he longed to see him restored to health again. The Bishop consented, but insisted on providing him with a guard of honour from his household. To his

Frank Smoczynski

Upper: A modern artist's conception of the original Apparition.
Lower: The same artist's view of Tepeyac Hill at the time of the Apparitions.

37

Frank Smoczynski

An early artist's impression of the Apparition.

Frank Smoczynski

Frank Smoczynski

Upper: A modern artist's depiction of the appearance of the Blessed Mother to Juan Bernardino, Juan Diego's uncle.
Lower: Bishop Zumarraga of Mexico City being interrupted by news that Juan Diego is waiting to see him.

Dr. Charles Wahlig

Dr. Charles Wahlig

Frank Smoczynski

Frank Smoczynski

Upper left: A contemporary portrait of Bishop Zumarraga.
Upper right: The earliest portrait of Juan Diego, part of a larger oil painting. This is considered to be the most accurate portrait of the visionary.
Lower left: Pope Benedict XIV (1740-1758), a great patron of Guadalupe. He pronounced December 12 a holy day of obligation for Mexico, decreed a special Mass in honor of Our Lady of Guadalupe, and named her Patroness of Mexico.
Lower right: A contemporary artist's depiction of the Miracle of the Image in the presence of Bishop Zumarraga.

Frank Smoczynski

Juan Diego praying, from a painting by an anonymous 18th-century artist. It hangs in the sacristy of the parochial church of Guadalupe.

41

Opposite: Full-length picture of the Image.

Above: Bust-size reproduction of the same picture. (Below the right eye there seems to be a tear. This does not appear on the Sacred Image, but is the shadow of a slight mark present on the protective glass when this picture was taken.)

Frank Smoczynski

The translation of the Image to the first chapel at the base of Tepeyac Hill,
painted by Rev. Gonzalo Carrasco, S.J. During the transferal ceremonies,
an Indian was killed by a stray arrow, but he was brought back to life when
he was laid before the Image and the people prayed for a miracle. (Original
in the Basilica of Guadalupe.)

bewilderment, Juan found himself returning home to his humble village in triumph like a national hero.

On reaching Tolpetlac, he was overjoyed to find his uncle well again and resting outside the door of his house. The old man rose to his feet in amazement at the sight of his nephew surrounded by a throng of admiring caballeros and friars. A crowd of villagers quickly gathered round and Juan related everything that had happened. His uncle nodded as though he was already aware of the story, and then proceeded to disclose an astonishing epilogue of his own. After his nephew had departed to call a priest, he had become too weak to drink the medicine which had been left by his bedside, and he felt that his last moments had arrived. Suddenly the room was flooded with light and a beautiful Lady appeared to him, all radiant with peace and love. Juan Bernardino immediately felt that his body had recovered from the fever and, rising from his bed, fell on his knees before the celestial vision. The Lady told him that she had intercepted his nephew and sent him to the Bishop with her sacred image imprinted on his *tilma*. She had then revealed the title by which she wished to be known in the future, and of which he was to apprise the Bishop.

The interpreter who rendered the words of the title for the Bishop thought that Juan Bernardino was trying to say: "The Ever Virgin, Holy Mary of Guadalupe." Zumárraga was astounded, for the name Guadalupe had no connection whatever with Mexico, but was the name of a famous Marian shrine in distant Spain.

This shrine, situated in Estremadura, a province in the eastern sierra of Spain, existed centuries before the apparitions at Tepeyac, and a short digression into its background will help us to understand why the Bishop's interpreter assumed that Our Lady had identified herself with the name of Guadalupe.

The statue at the Spanish shrine represents the Blessed Virgin holding the Child Jesus in one hand and a crystal sceptre in the other to signify her Divine Motherhood. The image had a chequered history. Tradition relates that it was venerated by Pope St. Gregory the Great in his private oratory and that eventually he made a gift of it to his friend St. Leander, Bishop of Seville. It was venerated at Seville until the Moorish invasion of 711 A.D. when, fearing for its safety, some clergymen who were fleeing from the Moors concealed it in an iron casket, which was then hidden in a cave. In 1326 Our Lady is said to have appeared to a herdsman, Gil Cordero, and told him where the statue and its authenticating documents would be found. The cave was located on the banks of the River Guadalupe, a word which means literally Wolf River,[6] probably because that part of the country had been infested with wolves in the past. In 1340 King Alfonso XI of Castille ordered the erection of the Royal Monastery of Guadalupe, to house the statue, and placed it in charge of the Franciscans. Before long, the monastery became the most celebrated shrine in Spain, attracting ceaseless multitudes of pilgrims. It is, perhaps, significant that Christopher Columbus prayed there before embarking on his momentous voyage of discovery and that, in token of his gratitude for surviving shipwreck on his return journey to Spain, he named the island that had providentially saved him, Guadalupe.

Predictably, the early Spanish missionaries in Mexico spread devotion to their Virgin de Guadalupe wherever they travelled, and quite probably it was this fervent veneration which caused a misunderstanding regarding the name of the apparition which Juan Bernardino had given to Bishop Zumárraga. The word Guadalupe cannot be spelt or pronounced in Nahuatl, the Aztec language which Our Lady used and the only tongue known to Juan Bernardino, since the letters D and G do not exist in it. Therefore the inescapable conclusion is that she identified herself with a name that was *phonetically* similar to Guadalupe. The Bishop understandably thought that the Mexican was attempting to pronounce the word *Guadalupe* and the name was accordingly adopted for the new shrine and cult. There were many precedents to account for this corruption in translation, particularly among Mexican place names to which the Spaniards had simply given their phonetic equivalent.

Historical evidence is not lacking to show that at first the Mexican Indians were reluctant to accept the name of a Spanish shrine for their beloved Madonna, despite the fact that it was formally imposed in the 1560s, and that instead they used names of their own invention. For example, we learn from the Indian historical codices that even up to the end of the sixteenth century the natives did not normally use the name Guadalupe: on the contrary, they called the shrine Tonantzin and other pseudo-pagan names which, as we have seen, was the cause of considerable friction in the early Mexican Church. In one account of the apparitions, known as the *Inin Huey Tlamahuizoltzin ("Behold a great wonder")* and which historians believe may antedate the *Nican Mopohua,* the name of Guadalupe is significantly missing. Through its absence, the data in the Indian codices is confirmed.

Becarra Tanco, the man who played a dominant role in the Apostolic Proceedings of 1666, wrote that the name Guadalupe had long been the subject of question in the winds of scholars and he concluded that Our Lady had actually used the phonetically similar Aztec world *Tequantlaxopeuh* (pronounced Tequetalope), which means "Who saves us from the Devourer." At that time, the Devourer signified both Satan and the terrible pagan god.[7] Father Florencia concurred with this view in his concise history of the apparitions *Estrella del Norte,* published in 1688. In other words, Our Lady was identifying herself as the Immaculate Conception, the One would vanquish Satan. It is known that Bishop Zumárraga wrote to Cortes on 24 December 1531, inviting the Conqueror to participate in the triumphant procession which bore the sacred image from the capital to the first hermitage, and that he referred to the picture of Our Lady as the Immaculate Conception. From this, we may conclude that the Bishop was subsequently corrected in his misunderstanding, though we have no record in proof of this, and certainly the title Immaculate Conception was never formally substituted for that of Guadalupe.

The mystery had still not been fully cleared up when in 1895, Professor D. Mariano Jacabo Rojas, head of the department of Nahuatl in the National Museum of Archaeology, History and Ethnography, undertook an intensive scientific study of the word Guadalupe. His conclusion was that the Virgin used the word *Coatlaxopeuh,* which means "she who breaks, stamps or crushes the serpent", and which again was the equivalent of the Immaculate Conception. His verdict was corroborated by two independent authorities in 1936 and 1953. After a further exhaustive study of the matter, a Belgian Jesuit wrote a comprehensive book in 1931 entitled *La Nacionalidad Mexicano y la Virgen de Guadalupe,* in which he stressed that it was to be expected that Our Lady would give Juan Bernardino a message of such transcendental importance in his own language, so that he could remember the words and accurately repeat them, instead of a message containing an Arabic word like Guadalupe which could not be spelt or pronounced in Nahuatl. We must also note that at the time of the apparitions, the Franciscans were preparing their converts for the feast of the Immaculate Conception. In their sermons they used to refer to her as "she who crushes the serpent", knowing that this would make a deep impression on them since it also signified the crushing of their frightful serpent god.

A recent study of the word Guadalupe was undertaken in the 1950s by the late Helen Behrens, one of this century's foremost authorities on the sacred image. She was assisted by the noted Nahuatl scholar Byron MacAfee. In her report she stated: "Neither Bishop Zumárraga nor any other Spanish prelate has been able to explain why she wished her image to be called *de Guadalupe*. The reason must be that she did not say the phrase at all. She spoke in the native language, and the combination of words which she used must have sounded like *de Guadalupe* to the Spaniards. The Aztec "te coatlaxopeuh" has a similar sound. "te" means "stone"; "coa" means "serpent", "tla" is the noun ending which can be interpreted as "the", while "xopeuh" means "crush" or "stamp out". Her precious image will thus be known (by the name of) the Entirely Perfect Virgin, Holy Mary, and it will crush, stamp out, abolish or eradicate the stone serpent."

The latter, as we have seen, was the dreaded feathered serpent-god Quetzalcoatl, the most monstrous of all the original Aztec deities, to whom 20,000 human sacrifices were offered annually. If this interpretation is correct – and many experts of Guadalupe are convinced that it is – then the Blessed Virgin was implying that she would crush all the Aztec gods, behind whom, of course, was Satan. This recalls Gen. 3: 14, 15: "The Lord God said to the serpent . . . I will establish a feud between thee and the woman, between thy offspring and hers. She is to crush thy head, while thou dost lie in ambush at her heel." In Apoc. 20: 2 the serpent is specifically identified as Satan. And her victory over the serpent is precisely what transpired. As a direct result of the apparitions, there ensued the greatest mass conversion to Christianity in history.

In conclusion, it hardly seems likely that the Virgin would have referred to herself explicitly as the "Immaculate Conception" since the dogma had not yet been defined. It was only after this dogma had been promulgated by the Church in 1854 that she publicly acknowledged (in 1858, at Lourdes) this unique dignity which God had bestowed on her. It is significant that in those areas of Mexico where Nahuatl is still spoken, the inhabitants still refer to the sacred image as Santa Maria Te Quatlasupe (a slightly easier form to pronounce than Te Coatlaxopeuh), instead of the Spanish version, Nuestra Senora de Guadalupe. One of the principle reasons why the name Guadalupe has become so firmly entrenched in the English-speaking world is that almost all our knowledge of the subject has come from Spanish, rather than from Aztec, translations.

NOTES

1. Juan Diego's pagan name was Cuauhtlatohuac. Many books translate Juan Diego as 'John James', but this is incorrect. Spanish names like Jago, Jimerez, Yago and Diego have all been loosely translated into James, whereas there is no true English equivalent of Diego. It is the Spanish form of the Latin 'Didacus' and became popular due to a Spanish saint of that name who was a Franciscan Lay Brother in the Canary Islands (d. 1463).
2. *Juanito, Juan Dieguito,* though a valid translation of the diminutive, cannot quite convey the exquisite courtesy, almost reverence, inherent in the Nahuatl suffix *"tzin"*. Thus did the Mother of God address herself to the lowliest of the poor!
3. In the previous century, the Aztec King of Texcoco had built a high tower without an idol, dedicated to the "unknown god, creator of all things", according to the chronicler Ixtilxochitl, who was also his descendant. This divinity was called *"Tloque Nahuaque"* ("that of our immediate surroundings", or "who is by, or present, to all things"), an extraordinary metaphysical expression of God's omnipresence. This god was also called *"Ipalnemohuani"* ("He whom by everything lives·") The Blessed Virgin revealed herself as the Mother of this God to Juan Diego and the Aztec people (cf. *Historia*, organ of the Centro de Estudios Guadalupanos, France, no. 3, 2nd term, 1978).
4. *Teocalli*, literally "House of God", (*teotl* = God, and *calli* = house). Teocallis were the name of the shrines which the Aztecs built on the tops of their pyramidal temples. Thus Our Lady asked for a *teocalli* to be erected on top of the pyramid-shaped hill of Tepeyac, where her Son, the true God, would be worshipped.
5. Our Lady's role as Mediatrix of all graces, which is underlined here, springs from her co-operation in the Redemption, since her *fiat* at the Annunciation was uttered "in the place and in the name of all mankind", to borrow St. Thomas Aquinas's celebrated words. In giving us the Saviour, she gave us all graces. Through her freely-given consent to the Incarnation, there took place that spiritual marriage between the Word and mankind so frequently described by the Fathers of the Church. cf. *Ineffabilis Deus* (Pius IX); *Octobri Mense* (Leo XIII); *Adjutricem Populi* (Leo XIII); *Ad Diem Illum* (St. Pius X); *Inter Sodalicia* (Benedict XV); *Rosary Encyclical* (Pius XI); *Mediator Dei* (Pius XII), among others.
6. Some authorities translate it as *Hidden River,* or *River of Light.*
7. cf. *La Felicidad de Mexico.*

III

THE CONVERSION OF THE AZTECS

THE following day, Juan Diego and his uncle were escorted in triumph to the Bishop's residence where they remained as honoured guests for two weeks. Meanwhile, thousands were flocking to the cathedral to see for themselves 'the Mother of the white man's God'.

It was a sublime experience to gaze on the silent splendour of the sacred image. The Lady's features, ineffably delicate, were those of a beautiful young girl, of olive complexion, with rosy cheeks and dark brown hair. The eyes, cast down in an attitude of humility, were so full of expression that they seemed more like those of a living being. She wore a rose-coloured garment overlaid with a fine lace-like sheath worked with an exquisite floral design of gold. A greenish-blue mantle covered her head and fell to her feet. The glowing beauty of her person, together with an indefinable aura of a supernatural presence, has captivated untold millions down to this day.

Four centuries later, the American author Coley Taylor graphically described the extraordinary visual impact made by the sacred image. "The more we look at it," he wrote, "the more miraculous it appears . . . When you see the seam, which is broken, you wonder how it hangs together. The expression on Our Lady's face is altogether indescribable. It is so tender, so loving, so human in her enigmatical smile, far more challenging than that of the famed Mona Lisa of Leonardo. Reproductions do not convey the gentleness and softness of the moulding of the lips. In some, the eyes seem to bulge and the lips almost to pout, but there is none of that in the original – the contours are all lovely. And the great feature is, of course, in the eyes, which do not look like the painted eyes in a portrait, but living, human eyes, with the proper eye contours.

"To me, the strangest thing is this: ordinarily, when one is close to a painting, the detail is sharper than from a distance. But with the holy portrait this isn't so. You can scarcely see the stars in her robe;

yet they are dazzling from a distance. And from the scaffold's nearness, her robe is not the greenish-blue one sees from a distance, but a much bluer and darkish blue. The pink of her gown is very pale close-up, but very rosy at some distance.

"This reversal of matters intrigues me to no end and baffles all of us. And it is, or must be, part of the phenomenon of 'change in size' one encounters when the painting[1] looms so large, mid-way up the Basilica[2] aisle and shrinks to 'normal' when you get close. That, too, is a reversal. And always there is the tremendous sense of presence, a magnetic graciousness that has never been my experience with any other painting, religious or secular, that I have ever admired and loved. And I have seen and studied and admired so many masterpieces in my twenty-five years in New York – El Greco's, Goya's, Leonardo's, Michelangelo's, Raphael's, Verneer's, Holbein's, Rembrandt's, Raeburn's, Titian's – in the permanent collection of the museums, in private collections, and in the great loan exhibition for the World's Fair. There is nothing comparable to Our Lady's portrait. She left something of her presence with it, that is all I can say.

"Another thing we have all noticed – her face seems to be 'poorly lighted'. It isn't. I think she keeps it shadowed a little – perhaps out of modesty – no lady likes to be stared at. And this, too, is another reversal (so far as this picture is concerned). Her face is clearer in detail close-up, but veiled in shadow even when one stares at it from the foot of the altar. It is altogether a paradox and a delight beyond words. And it is this gentle presence, this vicacious graciousness, this enigmatical radiance, that no artist nor any reproduction can capture. In some mysterious supernatural way, she is still here at Tepeyac . . ."[3]

It has been suggested that in her dress and in her countenance, Our Lady does not have the appearance of a Mexican, but of a Jewess.[4] Mexican women, both rich and poor, wore short-sleeved, square-necked blouses, and skirts that reached well below the knee. The robes on the sacred image, however, are full length, as used in winter by both Arab and Jewish women in Palestine. Since fashions have changed little in the Holy Land over the past 2,000 years, one is tempted to speculate that the picture of Our Lady of Guadalupe represents her much as she actually looked on earth, though of this we cannot be certain. However, it is worth pointing out that one of the Guadalupan experts, Fray José de Guadalupe Mojica, O.F.M., who supports the above belief, having previously conducted a great deal of research into the matter, has the distinction of being one of the only writers who suspected the existence of the painted additions on the *tilma*.

But it is undeniable that the Virgin radiates a sense of purity which generations of Mexican women have been inspired to imitate. Writing several centuries ago, Father Florencia, S.J., noted this extraordinary effect produced by gazing on the sacred image: "Let all women, whatever their rank, find in the picture of this Sovereign Lady a figure of purity and a mirror of modesty: let them imitate her decorous reserve and the fitness of her most chaste attire. From this picture, as from a reflecting crystal, there reverberate as many tokens of honour and spotlessness as of light and splendour. Let them learn from it what they should reproduce in their own lives, how they must correct their dress, and what they must forego so that they may give no scandal." [5]

The crowds who first gazed in awe and wonder on the miraculous picture spread word of the prodigy all over Mexico, attracting immense multitudes to the cathedral. Thousands knelt entranced before the celestial portrait, succumbing to the extraordinary sweetness of its power and drinking in the ethereal purity of its beauty. "For those who enjoy the bliss of feasting and beatifying their eyes with the sight of so sovereign an object," wrote Fr. Florencia, S.J., in 1675, "every other picture will seem like a blot." [6] And the historian Clavigero wrote in 1758 of the "favoured ones" who have "the immeasurable happiness of seeing the most beautiful, majestic picture of Guadalupe." [7]

In surrendering themselves to the graciousness of the celestial Lady, the pagan Aztecs were unconsciously being drawn by her to the feet of her Divine Son. As they gazed, captivated, on the supernatural loveliness of her features, links of enduring love and trust were forged, binding each soul to her as if with invisible chains of gold. "In this maternal presence," as Fr. H. Rahm, S.J., expressed it centuries later, "one feels the innocent simplicity and sweet closeness of a loving child." [8]

In the meantime, Bishop Zumárraga began to consider the erection of a suitable shrine at Tepeyac in compliance with the Lady's wishes. Already numerous pilgrims were mounting the rugged slopes to kneel and pray at the site of the apparitions. It was imperative that a temporary chapel be built there without delay until such time as a more permanent and fitting edifice could be constructed. Large numbers of Mexicans and Spaniards were quick to volunteer their labour, and within two weeks a small stone chapel, or hermitage, had been completed.

On 26 December 1531, a triumphant procession conveyed the sacred image from the cathedral to Tepeyac. Through the closely confined city and out and along the causeway it wound, led by Bishop Zumárraga and followed by Franciscan and Dominican missionaries and a vast concourse of people. Excited crowds in carnival mood lined the city's narrow twisting streets; gaily decorated boats plied the gleaming waters of Lake Texcoco on either side of the causeway; while all along the flower-strewn route across the country, Mexicans in their thousands danced and sang amid pageant-like scenes of music, joy and splendour, waving green sprays and sweet-smelling herbs. "The Virgin is one of us!" they sang exultantly. "Our clean Mother! Our Sovereign Lady is one of us!"[9]

One group of Mexicans, in a transport of exhilaration, became so excited that they shot volleys of arrows into the air, and one of these shafts struck a spectator in the neck, killing him instantly. The dead man was carried through the subdued throng to the chapel at Tepeyac and laid before the sacred image, which had just been enshrined by Bishop Zumárraga. The vast crowd pressing in and around the little chapel instinctively prayed for a miracle. All voices rose in an imploring entreaty to the Mother of the Christian religion. Minutes later, the dead man opened his eyes and rose to his feet fully recovered.

Gasps of amazement were followed by an explosion of indescribable joy. Spaniards and Mexicans embraced one another spontaneously in a genuine manifestation of brotherly love. As the shock-waves of this further awesome demonstration of the power of the Lady reverberated across the country, the enmities which had poisoned relations between the two races gradually began to abate, although it would be a number of years yet before they finally died out altogether.

An ancient Mexican song, *Teponazcuicatl,* adapted to Christianity, has preserved the memory of that unforgettable occasion:

With delight I have seen the opening of perfumed flowers
In thy presence, Holy Mary.

Beside the still waters, I have heard Holy Mary singing:
I am the precious plant with hidden buds;
I was created by the One and Perfect God;
I am supreme among His creatures.

O Holy Mary, you live again in your picture.
And we, the lords of this land
Sing all together from the book of anthems,
In perfect harmony we dance before you.
And you, our Bishop, our Father, preached
Over there, by the lake side.

In the beauty of the flowers did God create you, Holy Mary!
And re-created you, through a sacred painting,
In this, our Bishopric.

Delicately was your image painted
And on the sacred canvas, your soul was concealed.
All is perfect and complete in its presence,
And there, God willing, I shall dwell for ever.

Who will follow my example?
Who will hasten to come after me?
Oh, let us kneel round about her!
Let us sing sweet songs
And scatter flowers in her presence!

Weeping, I commune with my own soul,
That the whole purpose of my song may be made known,
And that the desire of my heart may be fulfilled
In the building of the Virgin's house.
Then shall my soul be at rest there,

And it shall know perfume greater than the fragrance of
    flowers
And my hymn will rise in praise of the beautiful bloom
Which forms her perpetual adornment!

The flower of the cocoa spreads its fragrance.
The flower of the pomoya perfume every road
Leading to this holy place.
And there I, the sweet singer, will dwell.
Hark, O hearken to my hymn of joy! [10]

When the ceremonies finally drew to a close, Bishop Zumárraga
placed Juan Diego in charge of the new chapel, to which a room was
added for his accommodation. After making over his property in

Tolpetlac to his beloved uncle, Juan settled down at Tepeyac to devote the rest of his life to the custody of the new shrine and to propagating the story and explaining the significance of the apparitions. According to one of the earliest documents of the history of Guadalupe,[11] the Mexican who had been raised to life also remained at Tepeyac, keeping the little building clean and tidy as wave after wave of pilgrims flowed through its narrow doors in an ever-growing tide of devotion.

In explaining the message and the meaning of the visions to the pilgrims, Juan laid great stress on the fact that the Mother of the True God had chosen to come to the site of the temple of the pagan mother-goddess Tonantzin, which Cortes had destroyed, to signify that Christianity was to replace the Aztec religion. This startling fact made such an impact on the Mexicans, that for years after the apparitions they referred to the sacred image as the picture of *Tonantzin* (*"Our Mother"*) or *Teo-nantzin* ("God's Mother"). This sincere expression of their devotion was frowned on by certain missionaries, who feared that it might unconsciously lead them back to paganism.

Juan Diego's new-found apostolate has been graphically described by the late Helen Behrens: "When the little chapel, about fifteen feet by fifteen feet in size, had been erected at Tepeyac hill and the image had been brought there, Bishop Zumárraga put Juan Diego in complete charge of it. Then he went to Spain, where he was detained until 1534. However, he was sure that he could not have found a worthier or more capable person than Juan Diego to remain as the guardian of this great heaven-sent treasure. Juan Diego spoke the Indian language and he was a Christian. He explained the religion of the white men to the Indians who came to see the Image. He told them the story of the apparitioins and repeated the loving words of the Blessed Virgin over and over again, thousands of times, until all knew the story. When the Indians presented themselves to the missionaries, they had already been converted by Juan Diego. There is no other explanation for the astounding mass conversion of the Aztecs."[12]

Having initiated the Mexicans into the basic tenets of Christianity, Juan sent them on to the missionaries, who completed the work of evangelisation. As if by divine foresight, there already existed good means of communication in that vast country, the cities being regularly linked by swift couriers. In consequence, news of the wondrous events at Tepeyac and of Juan Diego's apostolate were soon common knowledge everywhere. And since Mexico was a land where art flourished, painted copies of the sacred image, accompanied by the story of the apparitions written up in codices, were circulated by the thousand from coast to coast, thus providing people with the nearest thing to a vivid audio-visual account of the whole dramatic story.

Until 1531, the Sacrament of Baptism had been administered mostly to infants – the innumerable war orphans were cared for in church institutions – and to the dying. The overwhelming majority of Aztec adults had resisted the advances of the missionaries since embracing Christianity would have entailed the abandonment of polygamy. However, as the cult of Our Lady of Guadalupe began to spread throughout the country, great numbers of all ages and classes began to long for a new moral code based on the example of the Mother of the 'white man's God', who could now only be the Mother of the True God, their "clean Mother", and who had captivated their minds and hearts with her radiant purity, virtue and love.

As a result, the few missionaries in the country were soon increasingly engaged in preaching, instructing and baptising. The trickle of conversions soon became a river, and that river a flood which is perhaps unprecedented in the history of Christianity. 5,000,000 Catholics were lost to the Church owing to the Reformation in Europe at this time, but their numbers were more than replaced in a few years by over 9,000,000 Aztec converts.[13] A famous Mexican preacher of the nineteenth century, Dr. Ibarra of Chilapa, graphically expressed this tidal wave of conversions as follows:

"It is true that immediately after the conquest, some apostolic men, some zealous missionaries, mild, gentle conquerors who were disposed to shed no blood but their own, ardently devoted themselves to the conversion of the Indians. However, these valiant men, because of their fewness, because of the difficulty of learning various languages, and of the vast extent of our territory, obtained, in spite of their heroic efforts, but few and limited results.

"But scarcely had the Most Holy Virgin of Guadalupe appeared and taken possession of this her inheritance, when the Catholic Faith spread with the rapidity of light from the rising sun, through the wide extent and beyond the bounds of the ancient empire of Mexico. Innumerable multitudes from every tribe, every district, every race, in this immense country . . . who were grossly superstitious, who were ruled by the instincts of cruelty, oppressed by every form of violence, and utterly degraded, returned upon themselves at the credible announcement of the admirably portentous apparition of Our Lady of Guadalupe; recognised their natural dignity; forgot their misfortunes; put off their instinctive ferocity; and, unable to resist such sweet and tender invitations, came in crowds to cast their grateful hearts at the feet of so loving a Mother, and to mingle their tears of emotion with the regenerating waters of Baptism.

"Our Lady of Guadalupe it was, who worked numberless prodigies of conversion to the Faith, with the irresistible attractions of her graciousness and the ingenious inventions of her kind charity . . . Hence she can say to us, with more reason than the Apostle St. Paul to the Corinthians: Though you had ten thousand preceptors and masters in the Faith of Jesus Christ, I alone, as your tender Mother, have engendered you and brought you forth."[14]

The missionaries were all but overwhelmed by the endless multitudes clamouring for instruction and baptism. Some priests had to bestow the Sacrament of Baptism six thousand times in a single day. One of them, a Father Toribio, recorded: "Had I not witnessed it with my own eyes, I should not venture to report it. I have to affirm that at the convent of Quecholac, another priest and myself baptised fourteen thousand two hundred souls in five days. We even imposed the Oil of Catechumens and the Holy Chrism on all of them – an undertaking of no little labour."[15]

Almost everywhere the missionaries travelled, entire families would come running out of their dusty village, entreating them with signs to come and pour the water on their heads. Others would plead on their knees for the Sacrament to be administered there and then. When the numbers grew too numerous to cope with individually, the missionaries formed the men and women into two separate columns behind a cross-bearer. As they filed passed the first priest, he briefly imposed on each the Oil of Catechumens. Holding lighted candles and singing a hymn, they would then converge on a second priest who stood beside the baptismal font. While the Sacrament of Baptism was being administered, the columns would slowly wind back to the first priest, who annointed them with chrism. Then the husbands and wives joined hands, and, pronoucing their marriage vows together, received the Sacrament of Matrimony.

Several trustworthy contemporary writers, including a certain Father Alegre, aver that one missionary, a Flemish Franciscan named Peter of Ghent, baptised with his own hands over 1,000,000 Mexicans.[16] "Who will not recognise the Spirit of God in moving so many millions to enter the kingom of Christ," wrote Fr. Anticoli, S.J. "And when we consider that there occurred no portent or other supernatural event . . . to attract such multitudes, other than the apparitions of the Virgin, we may state with assurance that it was the Vision of the Queen of the Apostles that called the Indians to the Faith."

Churches, monasteries, convents, hospitals, schools and workshops sprang up all over the country in the wake of this phenomenal missionary conquest. In 1552 the University of Mexico (now the largest in the world) was established by papal and royal decree and placed on an equal footing with the celebrated University of Salamanca in Spain. New episcopal sees were founded, and before long Catholic Mexico was sending native-born missionaries abroad, especially to Florida, California and far-off Japan, where their glorious martyrs, St. Philip of Jesus and his Companions, suffered for the Faith in 1597.

Meanwhile, Juan Diego continued in charge of the little hermitage of Tepeyac, living a life of great austerity and humilty. The sacred image was enthroned over the tiny altar and Juan must have spent long hours before it in prayerful contemplation. The bishop granted him permission to receive Communion three times a week – an almost unheard-of privilege in those days. "His face and form seemed to take on a new dignity," wrote Dr. C. Wahlig, O.D. "His frugality and discipline revealed the refinement of an ascetic. He had come to be revered as a man of great culture and lofty thinking, as befits a man who led such a holy life."[18]

At the Information Process in 1666, a witness, whose grand-parents had probably known Juan Diego quite well, testified as follows: "They saw him constantly occupied with the affairs of God. He went most punctually to the devotions and to the divine offices, in which he frequently took part himself. The Indians of his time held him to be a holy man. They called him the *pilgrim,* because they always saw him going alone . . . The natives very frequently went to see him and asked him to intercede for them with the Most Holy Virgin . . . for all held him to be a holy man, since to him and to no one else had the Virgin appeared. Moreover, they always found him very contrite, doing many penances."[19]

At some time between 1544 and 1548, according to the calculations of the historians, Bishop Zumárraga arrived at the hermitage and asked Juan to show him the exact location of the fourth apparition. The seer led the bishop around the shoulder of Tepeyac, and as he hesitated, trying to recollect where the Lady had intercepted him when he was hurrying to fetch a priest for his sick uncle, a spring suddenly gushed forth from the ground a short distance away. Juan then remembered that it was on this exact spot that she had spoken to him and asked him to climb the hill to gather flowers for the bishop.

The water was, and still is, clean and odorous, although not pleasant to taste, being slightly acid. The pilgrims were quick to regard it as having come from the Blessed Virgin and many of the sick claimed cures after drinking it or anointing their bodies with it. In 1582 an English traveller, Miles Phillips, recorded that "There are cold baths here where the water flows as though it were boiling; it is slightly brackish to taste, but very good for those who wash their wounds or sores in it. According to what is said, many people have been cured through it." [20]

Three centuries later, a French rationalist called Eugene Boban wrote: "The spring (of Guadalupe) is to be found in the centre of a little chapel of very interesting Moorish style. A crowd, armed with vases and bottles of every size and shape, were gathered around in order to draw this miraculous water at its source, just like Lourdes water, and they take it to cure all illnesses." [21]

An interesting sequel to the above is afforded by Brother Bruno Bonnet-Eymard, an active member of the *Centro de Estudios Guadalupanos* in France. Referring to a visit to Guadalupe in December 1979 he wrote: "I brought some (water) back and shortly after my return, gave it to drink to a young man whose case was desperate. Today he is in perfect health . . . with no other intervention. Those of his entourage who know nothing of this, say that his recovery is inexplicable. I am not claiming that his cure is a miracle, but I am stating what I have seen and what I do see, in order to show, as Father Beltran said, 'the filial confidence' that one can place in the protection of St. Mary of Guadalupe."[22]

To return to our story: Juan Diego continued his apostolate at the hermitage while Mexico was enjoying the benign rule of the Second Audience headed by Bishop Sebastian Ramirez y Fuenleal. Exploitation of the Mexicans by Spanish soldiers became increasingly infrequent as the two races gradually inter-married and settled down together in religious and social harmony. The Bishop's rule was followed by the wise administration of the Marques de Mendoza, the first Viceroy, and then by a long line of Viceroys and Archbishops who were to give the country nearly two hundred years of political and economic stability and peace.

In 1544 Juan Bernardino died at the advanced age of 84, favoured, it is said, by another vision of the Lady of Tepeyac. On the orders of Bishop Zumárraga, he was laid to rest under the hermitage. He was was followed four years later by Juan Diego, who died on 30 May 1548. According to a pious tradition, the

Immaculate Lady of his visions, who had called him her "much loved son" and her "cherished little one," appeared once more to console him on his deathbed. Juan's room in the chapel became a baptistry while his uncle's house at Tolpetlac was converted into a small chapel. A commemorative tablet was placed on the wall in the baptistry, which read:

> In this place, Our Lady of Guadalupe appeared to an Indian named Juan Diego who is buried in this church.

Juan's venerable name lived on in the hearts and homes of millions of Mexicans. "Among the poor, fervent Indians," wrote Father George Lee, C.S.Sp., "the moral likeness to him is striking. Childlike, dignified, gladly mystic, they often have a personal intercourse with Heaven that altogether lifts them out of their paltry surroundings. They are blessed through the example and, I think, the intercession of Juan Diego. There are few more beautiful or more fruitful characters than his to be found among the uncanonised saints of the Church. No wonder that Mexican parents have long expressed their best benediction by saying: 'May God make you like Juan Diego.'[23]

Earlier in 1548, Bishop Zumárraga had been appointed as the first Archbishop of the New World. During May of that year, he undertook a long and exhausting journey to the distant town of Tepetlaoztoc, where he baptised, confirmed and married some 14,000 Mexicans. He returned to Mexico City seriously ill and it was on his own deathbed that he was informed of the passing of Juan Diego. He received the news with calm faith. He knew that he need not be concerned about the security of the sacred image, although its first faithful custodian was no more. Doubtless he turned with confidence to the Blessed Virgin and begged her to watch over it in the years ahead. Nor could he have doubted that one day a glorious temple, truly worthy of the Queen of Heaven, would be erected at Tepeyac. A servant brought him the news that Cortes had died six months before in Seville, with a prayer to Our Lady of Guadalupe on his lips. Zumárraga died just three days after Juan Diego had preceded him into eternity and into the presence of the Lady of Tepeyac.

NOTES

1. The word 'painting' is used here figuratively.
2. This refers to the old Basilica, since closed due to subsidence.
3. Extracted from a letter by Coley Taylor to Rt. Rev. Columban Hawkins, O.C.S.O.
4. This opinion has been put forward by Father James Meehan, S.J., in an article in *The Jesuit Bulletin,* April 1970, and by Fray José de Guadalupe Mojica in *Am I not here?* by Father Harold Rahm, S.J., p.69.
5. *Estrella del Norte,* p.166.
6. cf. *Estrella del Norte,* by Fr. Florencia, S.J.
7. Quoted in *Our Lady of Guadalupe* by Fr. George Lee, C.S.Sp., 1946, p.152.
8. *Am I not here?* by Fr. Harold Rahm, S.J., 1961, p.28.
9. *La Virgen del Tepeyac: Compendio Historica-Critico,* by Fr. Anticoli, p.45.
10. The *Nican Motecpana,* written shortly after the *Nican Mopohua,* records the translation of the sacred image from the cathedral to Tepeyac.
11. cf. *El Culto Guadalupano del Tepeyac,* by Fray Fidel de Jesus Chauvet, O.F.M., Mexico, 1978.
12. *Handbook on Guadalupe,* pp.20-21.
13. cf. *Indian History,* Tr. 2, c.3. by Fr. Toribo.
14. Sermon at Guadalupe, October 1895.
15. *Indian History,* Tr. 2, c.3. by Fr. Toribo.
16. cf. *La Virgen del Tepeyac: Compendio Historica-Critico,* by Fr. Anticoli, S.J., which recounts many anecdotes of the mass conversion of the Aztecs.
17. *Ibid.*
18. *Juan Diego,* by Dr. C. Wahlig, O.D., 1972, p.73.
19. *Our Lady of Guadalupe,* by Fr. George Lee, C.S.Sp. 1946, p.280.
20. cf. *El Culto Guadalupano del Teyeyac,* by Fray Fidel de Jesus Chauvet, O.F.M., Mexico 1978.
21. Eugene Boban, *Catalogue raisone de la collection de M. E. Goupil,* Paris 1891, t.II, p.199.
22. Recorded in *The Catholic Counter Reformation in the XXth century,* October 1980, No. 127. The reference to Father Beltran is from '*Treinta y dos milagros Guadalupanos historicamente comprobadas',* ed. Tradicien, Mexico, 1972, p.10.
23. *Our Lady of Guadalupe,* by Fr. George Lee, C.S.Sp., 1946, p.283.

IV

THE HISTORICAL BASIS OF GUADALUPE

BEFORE proceeding to recount the subsequent development of the cult of Our Lady of Guadalupe, it is important to pause and trace the historical basis of the apparitions at Tepeyac. This might at first appear superfluous since the reality of the visions seems incontestable, particularly in the light of the immense and far-reaching consequences they set in motion. Unfortunately, most of the original documents concerning the great event of 1531 have not survived the centuries, and rationalist critics have spared no pains in attempting to prove that the apparitions are simply a myth, that the miraculous portrait is no more than a painting, and that the cult of Our Lady of Guadalupe is either based upon superstition, or the product of an amalgamation of pagan and Christian beliefs.[1] It is symptomatic of our present disbelieving age that past events which point to an incontestably supernatural origin (such as the miracles of Christ and the wonders wrought by the saints), should be explained away as mere 'legends' or 'pious myths.' In the case of Guadalupe, agnostic intellectuals have exploited to the full both the paucity of original documents, and other factors such as the silence of Bishop Zumárraga concerning the apparitions, and the notorious sermon preached by Fray Francisco de Bustamante in 1556, denouncing the sacred image as an "Indian painting." Hence it is important to demonstrate that the apparitions, the celestial portrait itself, and the cult of Our Lady of Guadalupe are established upon a sound factual, historical basis; and this independently of the fact that the supernatural origin of the sacred image has been underlined by the most recent investigations of modern science.

The scarcity of the original documents relating to Guadalupe may be partially explained by the acute shortage of paper in Mexico at that time, for which there is firm evidence as will be seen later, but especially by the simple fact that the existence of the miraculous portrait enshrined at Tepeyac was so self-evident to the Mexicans that it probably did not occur to a race unaccustomed to making and keeping records of events, to set out a written documentation of the apparitions. Almost the entire history of the Aztec nation before the arrival of the Spanish is derived from posterior testimonies, gathered by the chroniclers of the Conquest, and from the transcriptions of indigenous codices which were copied several centuries later by Boturini, Gama, Pichardo and others, the originals having been lost.

While it cannot be affirmed with certainty how far these two constraints were responsible for the shortage of contemporary records on Guadalupe, it need hardly be pointed out that written evidence of a past event is not the only factor required to validate it. The value of tradition must also be taken into account – something handed down from generation to generation by people who seriously believe it to be worth preserving. "Indeed tradition in its best Church sense of all truth handed down *(traditum)* and all truth to be handed on *(tradendum)*, is the only complete history," observed Fr. George Lee.[2]

In the case of Guadalupe, traditional belief in the apparitions and the miraculous image has flowed broad and deep through the hearts of untold millions of Mexicans, from the middle of the sixteenth century down to the present day. And as we shall now see, the evidence for this living tradition is decisively upheld by incontestable, if scantily documented proof.

We have previously referred to the Mexican codices or picture stories describing the apparitions and accompanied by painted copies of the sacred image, which were circulated all over the country.

These accounts, in hieroglyphic form, were memorised by public chanters and declaimed to entire villages. With the advance of education, the story was translated into the Mexican *nahuatl* language using Latin characters. The earliest copy of this rendition still extant was found in the archives of the Guadalupan sanctuary in 1649 and although by then a whole century had passed since the great event of 1531, scholars were quick to recognise that its diction belonged to the period immediately following the apparitions. The author is believed to have been an Aztec nobleman, Don Valeriano, who was later to write a more comprehensive account of the story, the celebrated *Nican Mopohua,* about which more later.

Several other written references to the apparitions have survived the centuries, some incidental, but others with a much clearer confirmatory ring. The will of a relative of Juan Diego, for example, includes this passage: "By this means (Juan Diego), was accomplished the miracle there, over at Tepeyac, where appeared the loved Lady, Holy Mary, whose amiable Picture we see in Guadalupe."[3]

Other wills of the sixteenth century which are still extant allude to the shrine at Tepeyac. Bartholomew Lopez of Colima wrote on 15 November 1537: "I request that a hundred Masses be said for the repose of my soul in the House of Our Lady of Guadalupe, the cost to be deducted from my estate."[4] Further evidence of several witnesses testifying to the widespread cult of the Virgin of Guadalupe, prior to 1556, is also still in existence.[5]

Of cardinal important is an incontestably authentic document recently found in the Mexican records of the Bibliotheque Nationale, Paris, 6,000 miles from Guadalupe. It is the will of Don Francisco Verdugo Quetzalmamalitzan, Chief of Teotihuacan, dated 2 April 1563. "The first thing I order is that, if God delivers me from this life, four pesos in alms should immediately be given to Our Lady of Guadalupe, for the priest residing in the church to say Masses for me."[6] What is so remarkable about this testament is that it records an event in the *Nican Motecpana* (a document dated later than the *Nican Mopohua,* dealing with the miracles attributed to the sacred image), namely, how Teotihuacan escaped a severe repression following a local insurrection, through the intercession of Our Lady of Guadalupe. The date of this episode cited by the author of the will differs by only one month from that given in the *Nican Motecpana,* but the error, says Brother Bruno Bonnet-Eymard, "is a guarantee of the independence of the two documents, the one confirming the authenticity of the other."[7]

In 1790, Dr. Bartolache, the author of a famous book on Guadalupe, was able to decipher an entry in the Tlaxcalan Annals in the library of Mexico University. "Year 1531," it read, "to Juan Diego appeared the loved Lady of Guadalupe of Mexico, called Tepeyac. Year 1548, died Juan Diego, to whom appeared the loved Lady of Guadalupe of Mexico."

Within the same University, there also existed a very early manuscript recounting the story of the apparitions, of which a certain Dr. Uribe declared publicly in 1777 (at a time when anyone could have checked his story): "The history of this same (miracle) in the Mexican tongue, is today in the archives of the Royal University; and its age, though not known to the year, is recognised as running close to the time of the apparitions. This is made manifest, both by the form of the letters and by the paper, which is of agave, such as the Indians used before the Conquest."[8]

Writing in 1686, the Jesuit theologian Father Francisco Florencia, recorded: "Before the great inundation of the city (1629-34), the

Mexicans were accustomed to assemble in immense crowds, with festive dress and rich plumes, on the day on which they celebrated the feast of the renowned apparitions at the shrine of Guadalupe. Thereupon forming a circle that occupied the whole wide area before the church, they danced around to the music which, according to custom, two aged men produced on an instrument called a *teponaztli*. At the same time, and in a metre peculiar to their language, the musicians sang songs about the Apparitions of the Most Holy Virgin to Juan Diego of the messages which he bore from the Sovereign Lady to the Bishop, Don Fray Juan de Zumárraga, of the delivery of the flowers when the Mother of God gave them to him, and of the apparition, when he showed the flowers in the Bishop's presence, of the holy Picture figured and painted on his mantle or *tilma*. In addition, they chanted the miracles that the holy Picture had wrought on the day that it was set up in the first chapel, as well as the praise and jubilation with which the event was celebrated by the natives.'[9] Father Florencia may have seen this spectacle himself as a boy, or else he may have heard of it from his parents.

A complete account of the story of Guadalupe was apparently written and has been accepted as genuine, though the original copy has not survived. It was penned sometime between 1548 and 1554 by the Aztec nobleman mentioned earlier, who took the name Antonio Valeriano on the occasion of his baptism. An intellectual of considerable stature, he wrote his account in the Indian *nahuatl* language. It is known universally as the *Nican Mopohua,* from the first two words of the title "herein is related," and which reads in full:

'Herein is related in order and arrangement, the manner in which the ever-Virgin Mary, Mother of God, recently and marvellously appeared in Tepeyac, which is called Guadalupe.'

According to the late historian Padre Mariano Cuevas, Don Valeriano was born at Azcapotzalco in 1520, and was a nephew of the great Emperor Montezuma. At the age of 13, he entered the Holy Cross College at Tlaltelolco, only recently founded by Bishop Zumárraga. A brilliant scholar, he was the first graduate to take honours in Latin and Greek and eventually became professor of philosophy and dean of the College for some twenty years. He also served as a judge and then as governor of Mexico City for over thirty-five years, displaying exceptional administrative talents.

Since he was a close friend of Juan Diego and his uncle, he was able to record the story for posterity at first hand.[10]

Don Valeriano died in 1605 without leaving any heirs. He bequeathed all his writings to a distant cousin, Don Fernando de Alba Ixtlilxochitl, who in turn left them to his son, Don Juan. When the latter died in 1682, all the books and documents were left to a Canon of the Metropolitan Cathedral in Mexico City, Don Carlos de Siguenza y Gongóra. Upon his death in 1700, they were bequeathed to the Jesuit College of SS. Peter and Paul, according to Don Antonio Pompa y Pompa, director of the National Museum of Archaeology and Anthropology and official historian of Guadalupe. When the Jesuits were expelled from the country in 1767, the library was handed over to the University of Mexico. Unfortunately, during the occupation of the city by the American troops in the U.S. – Mexican war of 1847, the documents disappeared. After an extensive search, copies were traced in Mexico and in the Library of the Hispanic Society of America in New York, together with copies of the *Nican Motecpana* already referred to. Of the *Nican Motecpana,* we only know that it is believed to have been the work of a devout intellectual named Fernando de Alva, the distant cousin of Don Valeriano.

Writing in 1568, the soldier-historian Bernal Diaz, who had been a companion of Cortes during his campaign in Mexico, wrote: "Look at the Holy House of Our Lady of Guadalupe . . . and see the holy miracles that it has worked and is working every day."[11] And twenty-one years later, Suarez de Peralta noted the arrival of the Viceroy at the shrine in his *Sketches of New Spain:* 'He came to Our Lady of Guadalupe which is a picture of very great devotion, six miles from Mexico City. It has wrought many miracles and to this devotion the whole land hurried . . ."

During the middle of the seventeenth century, interest centred on the Juridical Acts concerning the visions and the chapel at Tepeyac. In 1640 the Public Records Department of Mexico City assured Fray Miguel Sanchez, a prominent author and theologian, that they were once in possession of these Acts. Shortly afterwards, during the Apostolic Process of Guadalupe in 1666, Sanchez testified that he had seen Dr. de la Torre, dean of the cathedral and the Archbishop of Mexico City, Garcia de Mendoza, "reading with great affection the Acts and Process of the said apparition." His testimony was later reinforced by the brief of Benedict XIV which was written in 1754 after an exhaustive enquiry into every aspect of the Guadalupe story. In acknowledging that the Juridical Acts had been lost, His Holiness added: "It is certain that they once existed."

From all this it is evident that, despite the paucity of original documents, belief in the apparitions of Our Lady at Tepeyac rests on a firm historical basis, complemented by an undying tradition of the great event in the hearts of the Mexican people. As Cardinal Lorenzana expressed it in a sermon at Guadalupe in 1770: "We regret that the Acts of Authentication of the miracle have been lost; but they do not fail us, for they remain written in the hearts of Spaniards and natives. When the event occurred, there was no secretary, no notary, no archives; and their testimony is advantageously replaced by the tradition perpetuated in the works, hieroglyphics and maps of the Mexicans."

Before we conclude this summary of historical evidence, an explanation is necessary regarding the silence of Bishop Zumárraga. At first sight this appears inexplicable, since the prelate was at the very centre of the sublime drama. The only letter he is believed to have written concerning the apparitions – at least, the only one we know of – was addressed to the Calahorra convent at Vitoria, Spain. Although this letter can no longer be traced, a Franciscan Commissary in the second half of the eighteenth century, Fr. Pedro de Mezquia, attested that he "saw and read a letter of the Archbishop to the religious of that convent, recounting the visions of Our Lady of Guadalupe, as and how they happened." Significantly, none of the Franciscan's contemporaries disputed the existence of this letter.[12]

Though to this day nothing further from the pen of Bishop Zumárraga regarding Guadalupe has ever been found, this is not to say that some writing of his will never appear, as unknown or long-lost documents appertaining to sixteenth century Mexico are still occasionally coming to light in the archives of a number of countries.

We have already alluded to the chronic shortage of paper in Mexico during the prelate's episcopate. Indeed, in the Brief of Benedict XIV in 1754 it was disclosed that not even a signature of Bishop Zumárraga had survived in Mexico itself. In a letter to the Emperor Charles V in 1538, the Bishop complained: "Little progress can be made with our printing through scarcity of paper. This is an obstacle preventing the publication of many works that we have prepared, and also of those that should be reprinted."[13]

However, there was a more cogent reason for the Bishop's almost total silence on Guadalupe, and one which incidentally resembles the silence that enveloped the Holy Shroud in the fourteenth century. We have seen that at the time of the apparitions, the Aztecs were on the verge of launching a general insurrection against

Spanish despotism. Zumárraga, as head of the infant Mexican Church and official Protector of the Natives, found himself caught between two fires: on the one hand, martyrdom at the hands of the avenging Aztecs, and on the other, the growing persecution to which he was subjected by the tyrannical civil administration. The avaricious conquerors did not hesitate to drag his priests from their pulpits and threaten them with physical violence when they dared to uphold the human rights of the defenceless natives. After the despot Guzman was desposed by the Emperor Charles V, passions continued to run high for some time, and they only gradually subsided under the influence of the warm rays of the vision at Tepeyac. Accordingly, Zumárraga was compelled to tread warily. He erected a chapel at the spot of the apparitions and quietly promoted the cult, but to proclaim openly the fact that Heaven had thus favoured a poor Mexican might have been interpreted by the authorities as an act of deliberate political provocation. So the Bishop exercised extreme prudence for a number of years, and to compound his problems, he was soon faced with a new predicament from an entirely different quarter, which arose in place of the now dwindling persecution.

A number of the missionary friars in the country had earlier been infected by Luther's misguided preaching against the so-called worship of images, and had convinced themselves that the passionate devotion of the natives to the sacred portrait at Tepeyac represented a perilous leaning in this direction. They were also concerned that vast numbers of Mexicans had been baptised solely as a result of seeing this sacred portrait, and not after thorough catechetical instruction and preparation in Christian living.

These fears were aggravated by the disquieting discovery that some of the newly baptised Christians still clung to vestiges of their pagan traditions, concealing idols beneath their crucifixes and surreptitiously worshipping them. "The missionaries would be told how idols were placed at the foot of the cross or on the steps under stones", wrote Father Chauvet, "to make it look as though they were adoring the cross, whilst adoring the demon. In the light of these facts . . they (the missionaries) stipulated that no cult of any image or particular shrine was to be encouraged or favoured."[14]

This iconoclastic and clearly heretical pastoral stance was the cause of much friction in the young Mexican Church. Had these missionaries reflected more prayerfully on the relatively few converts before the apparitions, compared to the immense numbers who flocked to Baptism as a result of seeing the sacred image, they must surely have recognised the evidence of a direct intervention by

God and that in consequence their duty was to direct their energies to a systematic catechetical campaign aimed at extirpating the last vestiges of paganism.

But the missionaries were a force to be reckoned with, and one can sympathise with Bishop Zumárraga and his decision, in this dilemma, not to espouse the cause of the sacred image too openly. His caution was, perhaps, justified in the light of subsequent events.

In 1556 the new Archbishop, Don Alonso de Montufar, who was not so reticent about the sacred image, preached a sermon in his cathedral in honour of Our Lady and her miraculous portrait, taking as his text: "Blessed are the eyes that see the things that you see." (Matt. 13:16). He reminded the congregation how, at the first session of the Lateran Council, "two things were ordered under pain of excommunication reserved to the Sovereign Pontiff. The first was that no one should defame prelates and the second, that no one should preach about false or uncertain miracles." In other words, the Archbishop was challenging those who might censure him for advocating the cult of Our Lady of Guadalupe.

Two days later, Montufar journeyed to the hermitage and told the newly baptised natives who were praying there "how they were to understand devotion to the sacred image of Our Lady, how they honoured not the tableau, nor the portrait, but Our Lady herself whose representation this was." The response from his opponents was immediate and shattering.

Later that day, the Franciscan Provincial, Fray Francisco de Bustamante, preached to a packed congregation at High Mass in the cathedral of Mexico City, fully aware that among his listeners were the Viceroy of the country and his magistrates. He openly lashed out at the cult of the sacred image because "it was very injurious to the natives since it fostered a belief that the picture, which was painted by an Indian, worked miracles and was therefore a god," whereas "the missionaries had exerted every effort to make the natives understand that images were only things of wood and stone and that they must not be adored . . ."

The Provincial's words caused a widespread scandal, and the very next day the indignant Archbishop opened a juridical inquest into the unfortunate episode, during which nearly all the witnesses sided with him against Bustamante and his vociferous supporters. During the following weeks, acrimony between the two factions grew so fierce that the Viceroy was forced to intervene and counsel moderation. Though Montufar was reluctant to initiate canonical proceedings against Bustamante, he withdrew the custody of the

Tepeyac hermitage from the Franciscans, which was about the only effective action he could take in these trying circumstances.

This regrettable affair, although stimulating an even greater devotion to the sacred image, proved that Zumárraga's earlier prudence was the wiser counsel. As a result, a mantle of official silence descended on Guadalupe, imposed, it is believed, by Charles V in Spain. This, in itself, would certainly account for the scarcity of original documents on Guadalupe.

Perhaps it is more than coincidence that a similar fate overtook the Holy Shroud when Pierre d'Arcis denounced those who regarded the relic as genuine "when the said cloth had been cunningly painted." Pope Clement VII felt obliged to intervene (in 1389) and enjoin silence on both factions in the dispute, while permitting devotion to the Shroud to continue on condition that it was considered a "representation" of the burial cloth of Christ. In consequence, the later transfer of the Shroud to the de Charney family is still veiled in mystery.

But the Bustamante incident is important in one respect: the proven existence of his sermon confirms that the sacred image was already an object of widespread veneration at that time, and hence regarded as of miraculous origin, prior to 1556.

NOTES

1. See for example *Quetzalcoatl and Guadalupe: the formation of national consciousness in Mexico,* by Jacques Lafaye, Gallimard, 1974. The author's numerous censures and conjectures were incisively demolished by Brother Bruno Bonnet-Eymard, a French intellectual, in *The Catholic Counter-Reformation in the XXth Century,* no. 127, October 1980.
2. *Our Lady of Guadalupe,* p.102.
3. Can. Vera's Contestación, p.439.
4. cf. *El Culto Guadalupano del Tepeyac,* 24, by Fray Fidel de Jesus Chauvet, OFM, Mexico, 1978, which records several other witnesses from the very earliest period prior to 1556.
5. *Ibid.*
6. Bibliotheque Nationale, Fonds Mexican, no. 243, fol. 11-13. The author owes this discovery to the keen eye of Brother Bruno Bonnet-Eymard.
7. *The Catholic Counter-Reformation in the XXth Century,* no. 127, p.21, October 1980.

8. Sermon, 14 December 1777.
9. *Estrella de Norte,* p.97.
10. A document has recently been discovered in the National Library of Mexico representing a petition by a group of Mexican citizens to Don Valeriano and validated by his signature. Dated 11 January 1573, the petition requests that members of the chorus of the College of St. Gregory be allowed to enter that intitution as students, and asks Don Valeriano to exert his authority to ensure that the poor send their children to the educational institutions established in Mexico by the King of Spain.
11. *Hist. Verd.* c.209.
12. *Escudo de Armas,* p. 329.
13. Appendix to the *Life of Bishop Zumárraga* by Garcia Icazbalceta.
14. *El Culto Guadalupana del Tepeyac,* by Fray de Jesus Chauvet, O.F.M., Mexico, 1978.

V

THE DEVELOPMENT OF THE CULTUS

DURING the following century, the little chapel at Tepeyac, known as the *Zumárraga hermitage,*[1] underwent several structural changes and renovations, but the delicate fabric of the sacred image remained exposed on a damp stone wall by the altar, where it was touched and kissed by literally millions of ardent pilgrims without incurring the slightest damage. The crowds pressing into the tiny chapel seemed to grow with each passing year and their faith and fervour were rewarded by innumerable miracles.

The opening of a larger chapel in 1600 (now the sacristy of the parish church), was attended by the Viceroy, the Metropolitan Chapter and other civil and religious dignitaries in the presence of the greatest crowd ever seen at Tepeyac. The name and fame of the shrine had travelled thousands of miles across the world; Guadalupe was now revered as the Citadel of Mexico and as the Cenacle of the New World.

In 1622 the chapel was further extended to become a fair-sized church and the sacred image was moved once again, still in a perfect state of preservation despite the fact that the delicate maguey fibre of which the *tilma* was made had a normal lifespan of no more than twenty years. The new building, according to the Jesuit historian Father Francisco de Florencia, "is of adequate size and beautiful architecture, with two doors, one facing east, on the side, and leading into a spacious cemetery whose walls are adorned by merlons, overlooking the Plaza, and surmounted by a magnificent cross of carven stone. The other door faces south, almost straight towards Mexico City, its great portal and two towers giving grandeur to its structure. Its roof is gabled, with panels delicately worked, especially over the main chapel, which is shaped like a golden pineapple, and where more than seventy silver lamps, both large and small, are suspended."

His description continues: "The high altar at the north has a retable made in three sections, and well sculptured: it is in high relief and gilded all over. In the middle of this, a tabernacle of solid

72

silver . . . which is even more precious because of its beauty than because of its monetary value. In this tabernacle is enshrined the sacred image, behind lock and key. A door with two panes of crystal covers the image from head to foot; beside it there are two rich veils or curtains, which conceal the Virgin from view when no Mass is being said at the high altar, and when there are no responsible persons present to watch over her while they pray. When this is the case however, many lights are placed on the altar, to show her still greater reverence and to further add to her adornment."[2]

Of the many reported miracles that were attributed to the sacred image during those early years, there is only room to recount a few of the more prominent ones. In 1545 a nation-wide plague of typhus, which had claimed thousands of lives, abated almost at once when a large pilgrimage of children prayed for deliverance before the celestial picture. In 1629 a disastrous flood inundated Mexico City, drowning 30,000 inhabitants. A devout lay religious, Sister Petronila, claimed to have seen a vision of Our Lady of Guadalupe propping up the threatened wall of the city. On asking the Virgin why she had not interceded with her Son to avert the calamity, she was told that the numberless sins of the populace had merited a far worse chastisement by fire, but due to the sister's prayers and penances, the punishment had been mitigated to a flood which would persist for four years.

The Archbishop of Mexico accepted the sister's story, which had been given under oath, and ordered the sacred image to be brought from Tepeyac to his residence in the city, accompanied by psalms, penitential rites and prayers for deliverance. The sacred image was placed in a felucca, the only mode of conveyance, and the journey undertaken in pouring rain, through strong currents full of floating debris and obstacles lurking just beneath the surface.

It was possibly on this occasion that the *tilma* was folded in to three sections, causing double creases across the lower and upper third of the Virgin's body. On arrival at the cathedral, which was half under water, the Archbishop, Don Francisco de Manzoyzuniga, promised not to return the precious relic until he could take it back "with dry feet". This he was finally able to do in 1634. Though the waters did not begin to recede for some while, the supplication of the people never faltered and when their prayer was finally granted, Our Lady of Guadalupe was proclaimed as the Preserver of Mexico and an account of the event, describing it as a miracle, was sent by the Government to Rome and Madrid.

This historic event has been vividly portrayed for us once again by Father Florencia: "The Archbishop of Mexico, seeing that the inundation was so great and so overwhelming that all the streets of the city were used as canals . . . that many houses were submerged, with great danger to the people who dwelt therein; and that the flood went on and on, growing greater and greater every day, while no human endeavours sufficed to avert the dangers which all were suffering – seeing all this, the Archbishop decided that the only remedy was an appeal to God, who had laid a heavy hand on Mexico by sending this affliction, but who might be persuaded to remove it through the intercession of His merciful Mother, whose miraculous image had been like a rainbow of serenity from the days of the apparitions onwards, and who therefore might prevail against the overflow of the lakes.

"Having taken consultation with the Viceroy, the Marqués of Cerralvo, and with the Court and Chapter of the Cathedral, the Archbishop determined, after mature deliberation, to remove the image from its church and to bring it to Mexico City. In consequence, the two Princes (the Archbishop and the Viceroy), the Judges, the Chapter Members, and a great concourse of Mexicans, went forth from the city in a flotilla of canoes, feluccas and gondolas, richly adorned and preceded by torches and tapers. Propelled by oars, they set out for the sanctuary, for it was not possible to go by land. They removed the Virgin from above the altar where she had been enthroned during the last hundred years or so, and installing her in the felucca of the Archbishop, together with the most important personages in his retinue, they rowed her into Mexico City. There was a great display of lights in all the vessels, and music from bugles and flageolets. The choir of the Cathedral also sang psalms and hymns, but with more harmony than joy, because though they were full of trust in the company of the Virgin, from whom they hoped for a remedy, they were not altogether happy.

"When the flotilla had arrived at a short distance from the parish church of Saint Catherine the Martyr, that wise and prudent maiden, in the person of her statue, went out to receive the Blessed Lady . . . She embarked on the vessel and accompanied the Virgin for the remainder of the journey, afterwards receiving her in the church which was her own home, where the distinguished visitor was entertained with affectionate and reverend demonstrations on the part of the clergy, who were likewise richly robed for the occasion; and from the church she proceeded to the episcopal palace, the birthplace of the miraculous image, where she was hospitably received for the night."[3]

It has recently been suggested that during its five-year sojourn in the city, additional designs were painted onto the sacred image, possibly to mask damage to the *tilma* from water,[4] and that it was the Franciscan Fray Miguel Sanchez, a celebrated preacher and theologian of the time, who was responsible for making these additions. In an essay on Guadalupe, he identified the Virgin with the Woman of the Apocalypse, standing on the moon and bearing a child (Apoc. 12: 1-2). This, admittedly, is how we see the sacred image today, for the crescent moon appears at her feet and the tassels are indicative of pregnancy.

Sanchez certainly managed to convey the impression that he had arranged for the celestial portrait to be touched up in order to conform to the description of the Woman of the Apocalypse. At the end of his essay, he acknowledged that he had relied upon the teaching of Ecclesiasticus 38:28. This chapter deals with manual crafts as contrasted with the office of the scribe who procures wisdom. Verse 28 describes workers and artisans "who make graven seals, and by continual diligence, vary the figure: they shall give their mind to the resemblance of the picture." Likewise verse 31 describes the smith: "He setteth his mind to finish his work and his watching to polish them to perfection."

However, this theory is untenable, since we now know exactly what the sacred image looked like sixty years *before* the flood. In 1570, the Archbishop of Mexico ordered an exact copy of the picture to be painted and sent to Phillip II in Spain. The King gave it to Admiral Andrea Doria, where it was placed in his cabin during the victorious battle of Lepanto in 1571 – a battle of decisive importance in safeguarding Christian Europe from the threat of the Turks. After remaining in the Doria family for several centuries, it was donated in 1811 by Cardinal Doria to the growing shrine of Our Lady of Guadalupe at San Stefano d'Aveto, Italy, where it remains an object of veneration to this day. Thus in looking at this copy, we are able to peer back four hundred years into the past and see the sacred image exactly as it looked in Mexico in 1570.

Now the Aveto copy incorporates all the elements which, it has recently been suggested, were executed on the original sacred image decades *after* 1570! Hence, if there are painted additions on the sacred image – and that is still a doubtful question – they could only have been executed sometime between 1532 and 1569. Perhaps Sanchez did tamper with the image, but the most he could have done was to make minor amendments, such as shortening the fingers to make them appear more Mexican and possibly adding a border of cherubs (which was subsequently washed off, despite great risk to the frail fabric.)

As for the suggestion that the *tilma* may have sustained damage due to the action of water during the flood, the fact is that it had already proved itself to be amazingly resistant to more damaging elements than water. For long decades, it had been exposed to the ruinous pollution of myriads of votive candles burning beneath it. The *tilma's* frail ayate material (which normally rots after twenty years or so), had earlier been handled by countless venerating hands and touched by a host of various objects including swords, yet to this day it remains in a perfect state of preservation. And long after the great flood, the *tilma* was to resist the fatal bite of acid accidentally spilt across its delicate surface, and even more incredibly, the searing blast of a large bomb that was exploded immediately beneath it. Hence the hypothesis of damage by water is simply untenable.

At the risk of anticipating the conclusions to be drawn from the latest scientific investigation into the sacred image, recorded in the last chapter of this book, it needs to be stressed that the face of the Virgin, her robe and her mantle, have been declared "inexplicable to science". Certain areas that show signs of cracking are known to have been painted over to enhance the visual impact of the image. These areas comprise the sunburst surrounding the Virgin, the tassels, the fur, cuffs and white undercuffs, the moon with the cherub below it, the gold border on the mantle and the stars strewn across it, and the black brooch at the Virgin's neck. There were also one or two minor alterations, such as the shortening of the hands just mentioned.

Objectively, the effect of the sacred image on the heathen Aztecs was to reinforce the teachings of the Christian missionaries. The Lady stood in front of the sun; the Aztecs, who well knew how to read pictographs, therefore realised that she was greater than the dreaded sun-god Huitzilopochtli. Her foot rested on a crescent moon, which signified their foremost deity, the feathered serpent-god Quetzalcoatl, whom she had clearly vanquished. The blue-green hue of her mantle was the colour worn by Aztec royalty; therefore she was a Queen. And the stars strewn across the mantle told the Aztecs that she was greater than the stars of heaven, which they worshipped as gods. Yet she could not be God since her hands were joined in prayer and her head was bowed in reverence, clearly to One greater than her. Finally, the black cross displayed on the gold brooch at her neck was identical to the one emblazoned on the banners and helmets of the Spanish soldiers, as if telling the Aztecs that her religion was that of their conquerors.

To return to the account of some of the prominent miracles in those early days: in 1736 a terrible plague raged across the country, killing an estimated 700,000 people. There seemed no hope of deliverance from this new scourge, but when on 27 April 1737 Our Lady of Guadalupe was proclaimed Patroness of Mexico, the pestilence subsided, as if the proclamation had caused a healing hand to be extended over the stricken country. This miracle was to have a decisive effect on the development of the cultus, as we shall see later.

A further prodigy in the same year concerned a nun who was dying at the Convent of St. Catherine at Pueblo. On hearing the church bells in the city ringing to announce the joyous news that Pope Benedict XIV had proclaimed a special feast in honour of Our Lady of Guadalupe, this nun managed to withdraw from under her pillow a small picture of Our Lady and murmured: "Dear Mother, life means nothing to me, but in testimony of your apparitions at Tepeyac, I beseech you to help me." Before the bells had ceased their jubilant clamour, the nun rose from her bed cured.

Rome had taken an interest in the growing cultus ever since the time of the apparitions. As early as 1560, Pope Pius IV had installed a replica of the sacred image in his private apartment and had distributed medals of Our Lady of Guadalupe. Before the famous battle of Lepanto in 1571, a painted copy of the celestial portrait was taken aboard the Christian flagship as already mentioned, and together with the united recitation of the rosary, was firmly believed to have played a decisive part in winning that crucial battle, thereby saving Western civilisation from the Turks. About the same time, Pope Gregory XIII extended the privileges granted by the Bishop of Mexico to those visiting the shrine, and in the following century, Pope Alexander VII granted a plenary indulgence to all those who visited the shrine on 12 December.

The effect of this latter favour was to impel the people of Mexico. to press Rome for an even higher recognition of Our Lady of Guadalupe. Apostolic proceedings were accordingly initiated by Cardinal Rospigliosi, who became Pope Clement IX in 1667 on the death of Alexander VII. The hearings, which were held between 1663 and 1666, were aimed at gathering a sufficient weight of evidence to induce the Holy Father to grant canonical recognition to the apparitions and a higher status for the basilica at Tepeyac. All available knowledge and data concerning the apparitions and the sacred image, together with the testimony of many witnesses taken under oath, were gathered by an official commission under the chairmanship of the Viceroy, the Marquis of Mancera.

The depositions substantially broadened and deepened the existing knowledge of Guadalupe. The Painters' Commission, for example, testified that "it is impossible, humanly, for any artificer to paint or produce a thing so excellent on a cloth as coarse as is the *tilma* or *ayate* on which appears this divine picture." (The artists are here referring to the rough surface of ayate fibres; the image side of the *tilma* had inexplicably been rendered smooth at the moment of its creation, thus enabling painted additions to be executed on it later). They added: "The imprinting of the said Picture of Our Lady of Guadalupe on the *ayate* or *tilma* of the said Juan Diego, was, and must be understood and be declared to have been, a supernatural work and a secret reserved to the Divine Majesty." They concluded that what they had deposed was, to their knowledge, "in conformity with the art of painting; and for greater completeness they swear to it in due form of Law."[5]

Three professors of the Royal University were appointed to a special committee to examine the *tilma* itself. Their subsequent report, sworn to and signed before a Public Notary, contained the following statement: "The continuance through so many years of the holy Picture's freshness of form and colour, in the presence of such opposing elements, cannot have a natural cause. Its sole principle is He who alone is able to produce miraculous effects above all the forces of nature."[6] The professors confessed that they were perplexed by the strange smoothness on one side of the *tilma*.

Among the many witnesses, the testimony of Dona Juana de la Concepcion was of special value. Aged 85, she was the daughter of Don Lorenzo de San Francisco Haxtlatzontli, a historian and former governor of Cuautitlan, the home of Juan Diego. After giving her own account of events during the closing years of the sixteenth century, she disclosed that her father had been a meticulous keeper of records relating to the district, and that these included an account of the apparitions at Tepeyac in 1531, since Juan Diego had been a native of his village and well known to him. He had also known Juan's uncle, Juan Bernardino. Dona Juana added that when her father was fifteen, he had heard the full story of the apparitions from Juan Diego himself and had later committed to writing exactly what he had heard. Unfortunately for posterity, this record of Don Lorenzo no longer survives.

In 1666 the depositions were all forwarded to Rome, together with a copy of the *Nican Mopohua* which had been selected as the most satisfactory out of eighteen other accounts of the apparitions. Shortly afterwards, Pope Innocent X – the Roman aristocrat whose life was dedicated to succouring the poor – displayed a copy of the sacred image in the Apostolic Chamber.

Meanwhile, the people of Mexico felt once again that the existing shrine at Tepeyac still failed to embody sufficiently all the burning love they felt for the Blessed Virgin, and so they resolved to erect a magnificent basilica in its place as the finest monument which their artistic talents, skill and generosity could devise – a crowning tribute of their reverent affection for Our Lady of Guadalupe who had deigned to come into their midst. In 1694, a group of leading citizens of Mexico City requested the Archbishop to solicit subscriptions for the erection of the temple they had in mind. As a guarantee of their personal commitment to this dazzling goal, they immediately opened a fund with $80,000 of their own money.

After mature deliberation, the Archbishop gave his approval and all Mexico rallied to participate in this ambitious venture. It was quickly decided that the best site for the basilica would be the one occupied at that time by the church which had been built in 1622. Accordingly, the Archbishop decided to build a small church nearby to enshrine the sacred image while the basilica was under construction. This church was so well built that today it still serves as the parish church of the town of Guadalupe. In a ceremony of sumptuous splendour, the miraculous picture was translated from the 1622 church, and then the work of demolition began. The foundation stone of the new basilica was laid in 1695, and for fourteen years the work proceeded, at a cost of $800,000 without taking into account much material which had been donated, and the voluntary labour which was freely and lovingly given.

On 30 April 1709 there took place the imposing ceremony of installing the sacred image in its new home. On this great day, the Archbishop was attended by the viceroy, senior members of the clergy, councillors, judges and other public dignitaries, and the procession was followed by an immense multitude which stretched back three miles towards Mexico City. All the church bells for miles around rang jubilantly and the very air seemed to tremble with joyous emotion. The sacred image was enshrined above the high altar in three frames, the first of pure gold, the second of silver and the third of bronze, while the mounting was inlaid with solid silver. The ornate interior of the basilica glowed with chandeliers, colourful marble, silver railings, innumerable paintings, mosaics, sculptures and other adornments. It was the most magnificent

The enshrinement of the Sacred Image above the main altar in the Old Basilica of Guadalupe in Mexico City.

Dr. Charles Wahlig

Entrance to the square of the Old Basilica of Guadalupe.

Upper: The Old Basilica of Guadalupe and the Old Capuchin Convent in the background. In this picture one can see how the right side of the Convent is sinking.

Lower: A close-up view of the Old Basilica, which was dedicated in 1709. It held 5,000 people.

A close-up view of the facade of the Old Basilica showing a depiction in stone of the Miracle of the Image before Bishop Zumarraga. A large crack in the wall can be seen to the right of the relief and extending upwards alongside of and over the clock. This crack and others similar to it are the result of the building sinking.

temple in the Western Hemisphere. When the dedication ceremony was ended, there began a nation-wide novena in which religious and secular organisations vied with each other in spectacular festivities. Forty years later, the basilica was made a Collegiate Church and a Chapter of Canons was established within its precincts. The choir was renovated and embellished still further, and a magnificent organ installed.

All this time, the depositions of 1666 were surely, if very slowly, moving forward in Rome. From time to time there was desultory opposition. Despite the favourable attitude of Alexander VII and his successor Clement IX, the Mexican request that Rome should set its final seal of approval on Guadalupe and elevate it to a higher dignity by granting it a special liturgy, encountered objections from certain members of the court, who were opposed to what they termed "the canonisation of miraculous images." Other high-ranking churchmen in Rome felt that the honours sought for Guadalupe should first be accorded to the Holy House of Loreto, and that since Loreto had still not attained this singular dignity after centuries of petitions, Guadalupe would have to wait its turn. The debate went on for many years. After the death of Clement IX in 1670, a number of powerful supporters of Guadalupe disappeared from the scene and opposition to it stiffened.

In 1736 Mexico was ravaged by a plague of typhus which claimed 700,000 lives in eight months. In a desperate attempt to end the pestilence, the civil authorities appealed to the clergy to proclaim Our Lady of Guadalupe as National Patroness of Mexico. This was finally accomplished on 26 May 1737 by the Viceroy-Archbishop Vizarron, whereupon the killer plague immediately subsided.

This apparent miracle emboldened the Mexican people to urge Vizarron to reinforce the petition in Rome for a higher dignity to be accorded to Guadalupe, by the submission of firm evidence of the picture's miraculous origin. Vizarron agreed and appointed a special commission of the country's foremost painters under the presidency of the brilliant Miguel Cabrera, at that time the most celebrated painter in Mexico.

A thorough examination of the sacred image was undertaken by these experts. The report which they submitted to the Archbishop stated: "The plan of this holy Picture is so singular, so perfectly accomplished, and so manifestly marvellous, that we hold it for certain that anyone who has any knowledge whatever of our art must, on seeing it, at once declare it to be a miraculous portrait . . . Its consummate grace and symmetry, the perfect correspondence of the whole with the parts and of the parts with the whole, is a marvel that amazes all who see it . . ."

Cabrera later wrote a book on the subject in which he stated that the sacred image seemed to embrace all four types of painting – fresco, oil, water colour and tempora, blended in a physically unattainable combination. He also revealed that there was no sizing on the *tilma*, making it humanly impossible to paint on its rough surface. He could only surmise that the inexplicable manner in which the image side had been smoothed out was yet another part of its miraculous nature.

Having read this most positive evidence, as well as a favourable report on the sacred image prepared by experts in physics, the Archbishop decided to send a special envoy to Rome armed with these attestations, to appeal to the Pope in person, who was none other than the great Benedict XIV, one of the most learned men ever to sit on the chair of Peter. After careful consideration, the Archbishop selected Father Francisco Lopez, S.J., a brilliant intellectual and an eminent theologian who was thoroughly versed in every aspect of the 1666 proceedings. With shrewd foresight, Lopez took with him a splendid copy of the sacred image executed by Cabrera. Let the historian Dàvila recount for us the memorable audience that took place:

"Holding a rolled canvas in his hand, Father Lopez came before Benedict XIV, and having obtained permission to speak, briefly but eloquently recounted the story of the miracle of the Guadalupan apparitions. And while the Pope was listening attentively and wonderingly, the speaker suddenly stopped and cried out: 'Holy Father, behold the Mother of God who deigned to be also the Mother of the Mexicans!' Thereupon taking the canvas in both hands, as did once the happy Juan Diego before the venerable Bishop Zumárraga, he unrolled it on the platform occupied by His Holiness. Benedict, who was already moved by the narration, at this unexpected action and at the sight of the beauty of the figure, cast himself down before it with the exclamation that has since been the distinctive motto of our admirable and venerable Patroness: *Non fecit taliter omni nationi.* (He hath not done in like manner to every nation.) These words of the 147th psalm, applied by the Holy Father to our people, were afterwards introduced into the Office and stamped on the first medals."[7]

Eyewitnesses aver that the Holy Father was in tears as he venerated the celestial portrait on his knees. He reportedly told Father Lopez that if it were possible for him to journey to Mexico, he would make a pilgrimage to Tepeyac, *barefoot and on his knees.*

Overriding all opposition in the Holy Office, the Pope immediately composed a Mass and Office for the feast of Our Lady of Guadalupe and sent it to the Congregation of Rites, who subsequently voted for it. Benedict then formally awarded singular privileges and honours to the shrine of Guadalupe as well as a status that remains unequalled among the shrines of supernatural manifestations, surpassing even Lourdes and Fatima. He decreed 12 December to be a Holy Day of Obligation in Mexico, to be celebrated as a double feast of the first class, with Octave. He sanctioned the special Office and Mass and made them compulsory on all priests and choir religious. And with Apostolic Authority, he decreed, declared and commanded that Our Lady of Guadalupe be recognised, invoked and venerated as Principal Patroness and Protectress of Mexico. As a crowning tribute, he elevated the Basilica of Guadalupe to the rank of Lateran Basilica, making it co-equal with St. John Lateran in Rome, the church second in rank of importance in all Christendom.

That Our Lady herself seems to have been instrumental in this favourable turn of events is indicated by the mysterious resolution of an insurmountable difficulty which arose while the Congregation of Rites were considering the new liturgy. According to canon law, they objected, the request for an Office and Mass should have been introduced earlier, and by formal application to them. Father Lopez knew that this had already been done in 1667, but the documents had been lost. As he pondered his next move, he suddenly remembered that a prelate named Nicoselli had written a book in 1681 describing the registration of the request with the Congregation of Rites. After an intensive search, he was disconcerted to learn that there were no copies of the book to be found anywhere. He turned to Our Lady of Guadalupe and begged her to intervene and break the impasse. Days later, he was approached by a pedlar of second-hand books who insisted on trying to sell him one of his volumes. To the priest's amazement, he saw in the pedlar's hands a worn copy of Nicoselli's *Relations* – the very book he so desperately needed. Confronted with this unmistakable evidence, the Congregation of Rites speedily ratified the new liturgy and a few weeks later on 25 May 1754, Benedict XIV inserted the new Mass and Office in the Church calendar and issued his historic Brief "Non Est Equidem" promulgating all that he had decreed:

"To the greater glory of Almighty God and the furtherance of His worship, and in honour of the Virgin Mary, We, by these letters, approve and confirm with apostolic authority the election of the

Most Holy Virgin Mary under the invocation of Guadalupe, whose sacred image is venerated in the splendid collegiate and parochial church outside the city of Mexico, as Patroness and Protectress of Mexico, with each and every one of the prerogatives due to principal patrons and protectors according to the rubrics of the Roman Breviary; an election which was made by the desire, as well of Our Venerable Brothers, the Bishops of that Kingdom, as of the Clergy secular and regular, and by the suffrages of the people of those States.

"In the next place, We approve and confirm the preinserted Office and Mass with Octave; and We declare, decree, and command that the Mother of God called Our Lady of Guadalupe be recognised, invoked, and venerated as Patroness of Mexico. Likewise, in order that henceforth the solemn commemoration of so great a Patroness and Protectress may be celebrated with greater reverence and devotion, and with due worship of prayer by the faithful of both sexes who are bound to the Canonical Hours, by the same apostolic authority, We grant and command that the annual feast of 12 December in honour of the Most Holy Virgin Mary of Guadalupe, be perpetually celebrated as a holy day of obligation and as a double of the first class with Octave; and that the preinserted Office be recited and the preinserted Mass be celebrated." There followed a list of indulgences and privileges and the Brief ended in the accustomed manner: "Given at Rome, in St. Mary Major, under the Fisherman's Ring, 25 May 1754, in the fourteenth year of Our Pontificate."

The jubilation that greeted this wondrous news in Mexico can be imagined. Father Lopez received a hero's welcome on his return. Poets and preachers extolled the singular recognition and honour accorded to the sacred image. "Happy America! Favoured America!" they sang. "America beloved by Mary! O Americans, whence was this to you that the Mother of your Lord should come to you?"

From that day onwards, the image of Our Lady of Guadalupe became even more clearly defined as the personification of Mexico, and we must remember that by Mexico is included all the Spanish territories in Cuba, Texas, California, Arizona, Utah, Nevada, New Mexico and Florida. And as civilisation extended to the vast regions of the north and south, from the prairies to the pampas, so devotion to Our Lady of Guadalupe began to spread throughout all the peoples in these regions, and then in turn throughout the entire world; for had she not come as a merciful Mother, not only "to all who dwell in these lands" (i.e. the Western Hemisphere), but also to "all those who love me, those who cry to me, those who seek me and those who have confidence in me"?

During the Mexican War of Independence at the beginning of the nineteenth century, a copy of the sacred image served as their country's standard, leaving them on through many trials and setbacks to ultimate victory. The brief, tragic conflict between Mexico and the United States in 1847 was finally settled in a peace treaty signed in the sanctuary of Guadalupe in February 1848.

One of the most graphic accounts of the shrine at this time was penned by the Marqueśa Calderón de la Barca, the English-born wife of the first Spanish ambassador to the new Republic of Mexico. In a letter dated 1839 and sent to members of her family abroad (the letter was eventually published by the great American historian Prescott, a family friend), she wrote:-

"This morning we drove out to see the cathedral of Our Lady of Guadalupe . . . We passed through miserable suburbs, ruined, dirty and with a commingling of odours which I could boldly challenge those of Cologne to rival. After leaving the town, the road is not particularly pretty, but it is for the most part a broad, straight avenue, bounded on either side by trees.

"At Guadalupe, on the hill of Tepeyac, there stood, in the days of yore, the Temple of Tonantzin, the goddess of earth and of corn, a mild deity, who rejected human victims, and was only to be propitiated by the sacrifices of turtle doves, swallows, pigeons, etc. She was the protectress of the Totonoqui Indians. The spacious church, which now stands at the foot of the mountain, is one of the richest in Mexico. Having put on veils, no bonnets being permitted within the precincts of a church, we entered this far-famed sanctuary, and were dazzled by the profusion of silver with which it is ornamented.

"The divine painting of the Virgin of Guadalupe represents her in a blue cloak covered with stars, a garment of crimson and gold, her hands clasped, and her feet on a crescent, supported by a cherub . . . We afterwards visited a small chapel, covered by a dome, built over a boiling spring, whose waters possess miraculous qualities, and bought crosses and medals which have touched the holy Image, and pieces of white ribbon marked with the measure of the Virgin's hands and feet. We climbed (albeit very warm) by a steep path to the top of the hill, where there is another chapel from which there is a superb view of Mexico; and beside it, a sort of monument in the form of the sails of a ship, erected by a grateful Spaniard to commemorate his escape from shipwreck, which he believed to be owing to the intercession of Our Lady of Guadalupe . . ."

As time passed, the Mexicans, forever yearning to heap still loftier honours on their beloved Patroness, petitioned Pope Leo XIII to incorporate into her Office the story of the apparitions and of Our Lady's consoling message to all her children, regardless of race, and also for the exalted honour of having the sacred image crowned. This supreme act of homage would set the final seal of perfection on the peoples' recognition of Our Lady of Guadalupe as Sovereign Patroness of their own country and Queen of the World.

To acclaim Our Lady as Queen is to acknowledge the pre-eminence of her role as Mother of the Saviour, and hence her royalty by right. For if the Son is a King, then assuredly the Mother is a Queen. Such a proclamation is also a recognition of Our Lady's unique innocence, virtue and dignity as the Second Eve. The First Adam and the First Eve were 'Lords of Creation' in the material sphere: the Second Adam (Christ) and the Second Eve (Mary) manifested this dignity of royalty in the spiritual sphere. ("My kingdom is not of this world," John 18: 36). "The Most Blessed Virgin must be proclaimed Queen, not only because she is the Mother of God, but also because it was God's Will that she should play a unique part in the work of our eternal salvation," proclaimed Pope Pius XII.[8]

Nine years of delay supervened after the submission of this petition, due to certain difficulties arising from a false publication which made considerable notoriety in Madrid. The Mexican people maintained a prayerful, anxious watch during this tense period of waiting. Finally the Holy Father granted the requests and ordered that the sacred image should be fittingly crowned to mark his sacerdotal jubilee. To the acclaim of a joyful nation, the Mexican bishops resolved to implement this sublime act of homage on 12 October 1887. It is interesting to note that only weeks afterwards, a young girl knelt before the feet of Leo XIII and asked for another singular favour to mark his jubilee, namely, permission to enter a Carmelite Convent at the age of fifteen. Both events – the appeal of the Mexican episcopate and that of the future St. Thérèse of Lisieux – we're to exercise a profound influence on the Church in the future.

The Holy Father's letter to the Mexican bishops on this occasion read as follows:

"With complete satisfaction, We have determined to accede to your request, that We should enrich with some special additions the Office already granted by our illustrious predecessor Benedict XIV, in honour of the Most Holy Virgin of Guadalupe, the principle Patroness of your nation. For indeed, We are aware how close are the links that have ever united the beginning and the progress of the

Christian Faith among the Mexicans with the veneration of this Divine Mother, whose Picture, as your histories relate, an admirable providence made famous in its very origin. We know too, that in the Tepeyac Sanctuary, for the repair, enlargement and ornamentation of which you show yourselves so solicitous, the manifestations of piety increase day by day, since to that spot . . . devout and crowded pilgrimages flock from every part of the Republic . . . Since therefore, as you yourselves recognise, the most loving Mother of God venerated under the title of Guadalupe is the author and preserver of this great harmony of souls, We, with all the affection of Our heart, exhort through you the whole Mexican people to see that they always retain this reverence and love for the Divine Mother, as their most signal glory and a fountain of every blessing.

"With special regard to the Catholic Faith, which is at once our most precious treasure and, in these days, the one most easily lost, let all be persuaded and intimately convinced that it will endure among you in all its purity and strength as long as this devotion, entirely worthy of your ancestors, is fully maintained. Let them, therefore, grow in it every day, loving with more and more warmth of affection so sovereign a Patroness; and they shall find that the blessings of her most efficacious patronage will flow down daily more abundantly, for the salvation and peace of all classes in society . . ."

Feverish preparation were at once set in motion for the great day of the coronation. Nation-wide prayers were offered throughout the summer of 1887, the basilica was renovated and prepared with lavish care and exactitude, while wealthy women vied with each other for the privilege of donating their jewels to be worked into the costly crown. "The Coronation is the solemn plebiscite of the religious and social dominion of Our Lady in Mexico," proclaimed the Bishop of Colima shortly before the august occasion.'

Saturday 12 October 1887 will surely be recorded as one of the greatest days in the history of Mexico. Forty bishops from every country of the Western Hemisphere, hundreds of priests, and an incalculable number of the faithful assembled at the shrine in a spectacle that eclipsed even Queen Victoria's diamond jubilee a decade later. The entire population of Mexico City seemed to have gathered in the vicinity of Guadalupe, and for those unable to make the journey owing to the distance, special services were held in towns and villages everywhere to coincide with the hour of the coronation.

"All those present," wrote a reporter in *El Tiempo,* one of the leading secular newspapers," were filled with a veritable explosion of gladness, of exultation, of enthusiasm. Men and women wept for joy. All felt themselves possessed by the Christian faith, while their souls were filled with an indescribable sweetness."

Pontifical Mass was celebrated by the Archbishop of Mexico, and in his sermon the Bishop of Yucatan stated that "in choosing the Mexicans as her people, Our Lady constituted herself as Empress and Patroness of America. O happy America!" he cried. "O fortunate West Indies! O blessed Mexico! You, the Queen of Heaven chose and sanctified. Not only has she done to you as she has done to no other nation, visiting you with such love, such predilection, such maternal tenderness, but in the rich gift of her Picture, of this miraculous image of Guadalupe, she has left you the testimony that your vocation is her work. O all ye nations of America! Cast your crowns at the feet of your Queen and Patroness, as in Heaven the four and twenty Elders do at the foot of the throne of the Divine Lamb, her Son!"

After the Mass, the *Regina Coeli* was sung in exultation and the rapturous sound was taken up by the immense sea of humanity stretching away on all sides of the basilica. When the Archbishop raised the dazzling crown over the sacred image, he uttered these noble words: "As by our hands you are crowned on earth, so may we merit to be crowned by Christ with honour and glory in Heaven."

Universal rejoicing was the order of the day. Special coronation banquets for the poor were held in Catholic colleges in the capital, while throughout the towns and villages across the whole country, at the end of the special High Masses coinciding with the service in the basilica, there was a spontaneous explosion of untrammelled joy – orchestras, bands, festoons, bonfires, fireworks, colourful decorations – all were mobilised to express the peoples' intense happiness.

The secular newspaper *Gil Blas* summed up the peoples' feelings in these words: "All, whether believers or not, find something to love, and to love intensely, in the Virgin of Guadalupe. Against her in this land, no man blasphemes. She is the ideal, the light that shines above our strife and our incredulty. It was for this reason that Altimirano wrote the memorable words: 'Come the day on which the Virgin of Guadalupe is no longer venerated, and you will have the sign that the very name of Mexico has disappeared from among the nations.' "[10]

NOTES

1. The foundations of the first hermitage have recently been discovered by excavation.
2. *Estrella de la Norte.*
3. *Ibid.*
4. The hypothesis of the painted additions was first made by the 1979 infra-red radiation investigation. See Chap. 7.
5. *Hist. Comp.,* p. 29. Father Anticoli S.J.
6. *Ibid,* p. 133.
7. *Hist. de la Compañia,* t.I., c.5.
8. *Ad Coeli Reginam.*
9. Sermon at Guadalupe, 7 October 1895.
10. 12 December 1894.

VI

THE MODERN ERA

IN the twentieth century, the cult of Our Lady of Guadalupe has widened still further and produced some new and most interesting developments. In 1900 the Plenary Latin-American Council obtained permission from the Holy Father for the Feast of Guadalupe to be extended to all Latin America, and ten years later Pope St. Pius X declared her the "Heavenly Patroness" of these countries. Nor was her dominion confined to the Western Hemisphere. Shrines dedicated to Our Lady of Guadalupe had already sprung up all over the globe, especially in Italy and Spain.

The Italian shrine has a particularly significant history. When the Jesuits were expelled from Mexico by King Carlos III of Spain in 1767, they spread devotion to Our Lady of Guadalupe wherever they settled. A beautiful shrine was erected to her honour in the church of San Stefano, Aveto, at the foot of the Appenines, and all the region's inhabitants flocked to venerate it. Miracles were reported and the entire province was placed under her protection. Then, as we have seen, in 1811 Cardinal Doria donated to the shrine the famous copy of the sacred image which had been made in 1570. Pope Pius VI accorded the shrine the faculty of a Mass and Office proper to Our Lady of Guadalupe and added a number of indulgences to the devotions practiced there. In view of its ever-increasing popularity for pilgrims, Pope Leo XIII designated the altar of San Stefano a privileged altar, *i.e.,* one where, by papal indult, a Mass for a deceased person celebrated on it has a plenary indulgence for the deceased attached to it. In 1947, the people even erected a large statue of the sacred image on the summit of Mt. Maggiorasco (5,824 feet), the highest peak in the province and also in the whole Appennine range, and this site has now become another favourite centre of pilgrimage.

Two Roman churches are dedicated to Our Lady of Guadalupe. The cornerstone of one of them, that on the Via Aurelia, came from Tepeyac and was laid on 12 December 1958 by the Mexican Cardinal José Garibi. The church was entrusted to the Legionnaries

of Christ, a Mexican religious congregation which had been
founded seventeen years earlier by a Father Marcial. It was to this
church that the dying Pope John XXIII came on the occasion of his
last visit outside the Vatican. Prior to this, a statue of Our Lady of
Guadalupe had been erected in the Vatican Gardens, together with
a statue depicting the miraculous creation of the sacred image on
Juan Diego's *tilma* – a gift of the Mexican people which was unveiled
on 21 September 1939. On the other side of the country, the
Mexican Chapel in the hallowed shrine of Loreto is replete with
murals depicting the apparitions.

In Spain, a crowned replica of the sacred image glows in the
beautiful church of Our Lady of Guadalupe, Madrid, and every
spring the first roses to bloom in the city's famous El Retiro Park are
sent to the Mexican shrine in the name of the Spanish people.
France also pays homage to the Virgin of Tepeyac. The outdoor
altar in her honour at Lourdes and the superb mosaic of the sacred
image in the side chapel at Notre Dame, Paris, are well known, but
of even greater interest is the shrine of Our Lady of Guadalupe in
Abbeville. A painted copy of the celestial portrait had reached
France at the beginning of the eighteenth century and a Father de
Gouye, S.J. made a gift of it to his sister, who was superior of the
Visitation Convent, Abbeville. The picture was venerated by the
community until the convent was suppressed by the Revolution in
1792. Fortunately, the parish priest of the nearby church of Saint-
Sepulchre recovered it after the turmoil in a second-hand shop. It
remains in the church to this day, greatly venerated and surrounded
by four medallions, depicting the four phases of the apparitions.

Elsewhere in the world, shrines, altars or statues in honour of Our
Lady of Guadalupe have been erected in London, Stockholm,
Addis Ababa, and Nagasaki. A beautiful replica of the sacred image
marks the spot in Nagasaki where the martyrs (some of whom were
Mexicans) died in 1597. Among many other lands, Poland has
enshrined a splendid replica of Our Lady of Guadalupe at Jasna
Gora, the heart of that country's intense Catholic faith. On 3 May
1959 the Archbishop of Mexico, Dr. Don Miguel Dario Mirando,
assisted by Jerzi Skoryna, President of the Former Polish
Combatants in Exile, raised the national flag in the Basilica at
Tepeyac and consecrated Poland to Our Lady of Guadalupe. In his
address on that memorable occasion, Jerzi Skoryna declared:

"Trusting in the Queen of Heaven, of Mexico and of Poland, we
have come to the foot of this holy altar, to the throne of the Virgin of
Tepeyac, offering our beloved fatherland to her, imploring from the
depths of our hearts, peace, liberty, independence and justice for

the Church of Silence, for our country and for all nations which
suffer under the most cruel yoke of the atheistic and perfidious
doctrine of Communism. The Virgin of Guadalupe already has her
cult in our country, just as the Virgin of Czestochowa, Queen of
Poland, has many devotees in Mexico. We believe that there can be
no stronger friendship and love between our countries than the
friendship and love contracted through the Virgin Mary, Queen of
Mexico and of Poland."

Of the forty-four popes who have reigned since the apparitions
occurred, twenty-five have issued decrees concerning the sacred
image. On 10 December 1933 in St. Peter's Basilica, Rome, amid
scenes of great splendour, Pope Pius XI reiterated the proclamation
of the Virgin of Guadalupe as Patroness of Latin America, after
which His Holiness crowned a replica of the sacred image and
celebrated a solemn Pontifical Mass. His successor Pope Pius XII
broadcast a radio message to Mexico on 12 October 1945, to
commemorate the golden jubilee of the first crowning of the
celestial portrait by Leo XIII. The Holy Father, who had already
established nine shrines in Italy dedicated to Our Lady of
Guadalupe, ordered the sacred image in Mexico to be crowned
again and formally proclaimed her Empress of All the Americas.

"Hail, O Virgin of Guadalupe!" His Holiness declared. "We to
whom the admirable ordering of Providence has confided (not
taking into account our own unworthiness), the sacred treasure of
Divine Wisdom on earth for the salvation of souls, place again upon
your brow the crown that forever places under your powerful
patronage the purity and integrity of the Mexican faith and of the
entire American continent. For we are certain that as long as you
are recognised as Queen and Mother, Mexico and America will be
safe."

Pope John XXIII proclaimed a Marian Year of Our Lady of
Guadalupe from 12 December 1960 to 12 December 1961 and
extolled her as "the Mother of the Americas." The moving prayer
he composed exemplified his filial devotion and homage to her:

"Hail, Mother of the Americas, Heavenly Missionary of the New
World! From the sanctuary of Tepeyac, for more than four
centuries you have been the Mother and Teacher of the Faith to the
peoples of the Americas. Be also our protection and save us, O
Immaculate Mary. Aid our rulers; stir up a new zeal in our prelates;
increase the virtues of our clergy, and preserve forever our Faith. In
every home may the holiness of the family flourish, and in the
shelter of the home may Catholic education, favoured by your own
benign glance, achieve a wholesome growth."

Pope Paul VI, his successor, bestowed a singular honour on the shrine by presenting it with a golden rose on 25 March 1966, a privilege subsequently accorded only to Lourdes and Fatima. Today Guadalupe is the greatest Marian shrine in the whole world, visited annually by up to *twenty million pilgrims*. Day after day throughout the year, unending throngs from all over the world converge there. Silent and recollected, many cover the last few hundred yards on their knees. They constitute a fascinating cross-section of humanity – smartly dressed businessmen, labourers, office girls, factory workers, farmers, mothers with small children, straggling family groups, bent, grey-haired men and women, long-haired teenagers in jeans – the variety is endless. Many of the poor are dusty, tired and bedraggled after days spent on foot, but their eyes blaze with the fervour of their faith and love as they join the mighty chorus of praise: "Perfect and Ever Virgin Mary, Mother of the true God." Some bear colourful satin banners, and others splendid floral arrangements or simple wreaths to lay at the feet of the sacred image.

Over half a century ago, at the height of the persecution under the Calles regime, Father Miguel Pro, S.J., the famous martyr of Mexico, wrote of the pilgrimages: "Nearly everyone in the city filed past the blessed image of Our Lady. I could not tear myself away from such a sight. Thousands of people were advancing down Peravillo Avenue, either on their knees or barefoot, praying and singing – both rich and poor – the working class and the upper class . . . In no time our own choir was engulfed in the multitude, all acclaiming the Virgin Mary, Christ the King, the Pope, the bishops!"[1]

Every May, hundreds of thousands of little girls all dressed in white arrive at the shrine, each carrying a bouquet of flowers to lay in the vast sanctuary, to be followed in June by equal numbers of little boys. December brings immense pilgrimages of such diverse groups as balloon manufacturers and taxi drivers – the latter inevitably paralysing traffic for hours in the vast city. Afterwards, each cab, with its tiny Guadalupe shrine, is sprinkled with holy water by dozens of priests. Month by month throughout the year, colourful groups tirelessly perform religious dances before the Basilica in salutation to their Virgin Mother. And as each troupe finishes, they mingle with the myriads of pilgrims pouring into the Basilica like an in-rushing sea.

Bowed in prayer before the sacred image, the hushed concourse of pilgrims yield themselves up to that magnetic sense of Presence,

A view of the Old Basilica and the Old Capuchin Convent, showing a huge crowd typical of the throngs of pilgrims who visit the shrine on feast days.

Another view of the Old Basilica and the Old Capuchin Convent, with masses of pilgrims visiting the shrine. The colonnade shown here has been taken down.

that gracious motherly tenderness that seems to repeat to each one personally those moving words she spoke so long ago to Juan Diego:

"I am your merciful Mother, the Mother of all who live united in this land, and of all mankind, of all those who love me, of those who cry to me, of those who seek me, of those who have confidence in me. Here I will hear their weeping, their sorrow and will remedy and alleviate their sufferings, necessities and misfortunes."

"Today, as the tourist enters the always crowded Basilica," wrote Henry F. Unger in the early 1970s, "he is amazed by the beauty of the Guadalupe painting high above the main altar. I can remember the intense prayerfulness of the kneeling Mexicans as they crowded around the main altar, banked with great mounds of flowers. I noticed too that scores of Mexicans were moving into the adjoining Chapel of the Blessed Sacrament. The visitor could not but be impressed by the magnificent main altar in this chapel and the many side altars . . . I could hardly move in this chapel in which Holy Communion was being distributed every fifteen minutes . . . From all sides, Mexicans moved on their knees over the rough floor towards the Blessed Sacrament. There, often with outstretched arms, they poured out their hearts to the Eucharistic King. Clusters of small children hovered around a praying Mexican mother, her eyes rivetted on the Host. Other Mexicans were bringing armfuls of flowers and placing them at the altar rail. Still others were leaving mementoes of some cure obtained through prayers to Our Lord in the Blessed Sacrament . . . "[2]

It is the same pattern in all the world's Marian shrines. Mary leads the pilgrims to her Divine Son enthroned in the Eucharist. With open arms, she welcomes her suffering children, longing to embrace each one of them and to guide them to the feet of Jesus, who had also once lain in her arms. In this sense she can be called Our Lady of the Most Blessed Sacrament, "the most theological of all Mary's titles after that of Mother of God," to quote the words of Pope St. Pius X.

Nor is Juan Diego forgotten. One realises that Our Lady chose to appear to him who was the least of all, the lowest and last in the village, so that no one would ever feel excluded from her maternal love. An ecclesiastical committee is currently gathering documents and data to be sent to Rome in due course with a view to the introduction of Juan Diego's cause for beatification. The process has been necessarily slow since what little is known of his life is perhaps insufficient to satisfy the exacting requirements of Rome when considering the detailed life and virtues of a candidate for sainthood.

In a pastoral letter of April 1939, Bishop Manrique Zárate of Mexico City stated: "Juan Diego had the sublime experience of having gazed upon the exalted Mother of God, by whom he was so well beloved that he alone became the bearer of her message of love to the infant Mexican Church . . . This one consideration should be enough to make us decry the lamentable lapse which has been incurred by all Mexicans, and especially by those of us who, through position or social responsibility or status, should have been the first to strive to advance the glorification of Juan Diego." The bishop went on to recount the life of this humble peasant, and the moral and theological virtues which he practiced, quoting from the various sources in support of this data. He ended by calling on all Mexicans to pray for his ultimate glorification.

One of the greatest living apostles of Our Lady of Guadalupe, Dr. Charles Wahlig, O.D., of New York has played a major role in furthering the cause of Juan Diego. In 1968 he journeyed to Rome to petition Pope Paul VI to make a pronouncement on the importance of Juan Diego. Although circumstances later prevented the Holy Father from carrying out the suggested plan, he was enthusiastic about it and awarded Dr. Wahlig a medal for having undertaken "a very apostolic work" in promoting the cause. Three years later Dr. Wahlig wrote the first book on Juan Diego (see the bibliography), and in 1974 he was responsible for the formation of a committee to take the first steps in introducing the cause of beatification. He subsequently presented the vice-postulator for Juan's cause with 157 invaluable pages of documents painstakingly gathered from the Ancient Manuscript Department of the New York Public Library.

Juan Diego's role as a model of the lay apostolate has never been clearer than today. "Why," asks Dr. Wahlig, "was such a special favourite of the Mother of God, who played such an important role in the history of Christianity, neglected by the Church, while others who accomplished less were honoured? Why should the likeness of Juan Diego be perpetuated as an integral part of the sacred image, only to be discovered more than 400 years later?"[3] (Dr. Wahlig is here referring to the astonishing discovery of the images in the Virgin's eyes, which is fully discussed in the next chapter). The answer to this mystery may become clearer with the passage of time.

The manner in which Vatican II's Decree on the *Apostolate of the Laity* was formulated, however, conveys the impression that the

Council Fathers may have had Juan Diego in mind. Through this lowly peasant, the poorest of the poor, God demonstrated that everyone, regardless of his or her station in life, can respond to the Divine call to action and if necessary, under the grace and guidance of the Holy Spirit, achieve results that are truly monumental, such as the late Frank Duff, founder of the Legion of Mary. Our Lady said to Juan: "But it is altogether necessary that you should be the one to undertake this mission and that it be through your mediation and assistance that my wish should be accomplished." By accepting this mission, he became the model of all lay apostles.

Today, in the midst of so many pressing difficulties, we can learn to imitate, above all, Juan Diego's unwearying patience and perseverance, confident that if we but exercise ourselves to the best of our abilities in whatever field of endeavour God calls us, keeping in mind the priority of prayer and sacrifice, we shall not fail. "It is therefore up to you, dear sons," Pope Paul VI said, "to be ready to give generously the help which is asked of you for the inner renewal of the Church, for the reconciliation of all Christians, as well as the testimony of charity in today's world 'in order that the world may believe.' " And echoing these words, Dr. Wahlig, himself an indefatigable lay apostle, had this to say: "If the miraculous picture of the Blessed Virgin Mary is the signal for the Woman's final struggle with the serpent, it is also the initiation of the laity's participation in the apostolate of the Church as we know it in modern times, especially in that apostolate animated by union with Mary. Guadalupe is a striking example of the fact that Our Lady does not work alone, but uses human instruments totally dedicated to her in love, to accomplish her tasks."[5]

To return to our account of the shrine and its development: in the early 1970s, the people of Mexico were dismayed to learn that the much loved Basilica was in danger of collapse. It had long been obvious that the massive structure was slowly settling and tilting. When the surrounding lakes were drained many years ago, the underlying strata remained waterlogged, and as a result many large buildings gradually began to sink into the wet, highly compressible clay of the old lake beds. Civil engineers have worked wonders jacking buildings out of the ground or back onto it, but despite all their ingenuity they were unable to stop the relentless tilting of the Basilica.

Finally the Mexican President, Eccheverria, decided to construct a vast new circular temple nearby in which to enshrine the sacred image.

On 12 October 1976, the imposing new building was sufficiently completed to enable the sacred image to be transferred from the old baroque shrine. Costing some $70 million in 1975, and seating some 10,000 people, the great circular structure was designed to "spread a new criteria in the construction of churches," according to Father Manuel Ponce, Secretary of Mexico's National Commission for Sacred Arts. Understandably, the revolutionary design of the new edifice met with much criticism.

Curiously, as soon as the new temple was opened, the old Basiica ceased to tilt. About that time the Government passed a law requisitioning all churches in Mexico dating back to the Colonial period, in order to convert them into museums of religious art, of which the former Basilica was to become the first. However, such an outcry was raised that this plan had to be shelved and up to the time of writing (1981) the building remains locked up to prevent a popular clamour for the return of the sacred image to its much-beloved, centuries-old home. It is not for this writer to comment on the present unfortunate state of affairs, but one can surely trust that in God's good time, Our Lady will settle the controversy peacefully to everyone's satisfaction.

The greatest day in the long history of Guadalupe was surely 27 January 1979, when Pope John Paul II visited the shrine on his way to the Latin American Bishops' Conference at Pueblo. Offering his homage before the flower-decked image, His Holiness declared: "Ever since the time that the Indian Juan Diego spoke to the sweet Lady of Tepeyac, you, Mother of Guadalupe, have entered decisively into the Christian life of the people of Mexico."

And indeed, the Holy Father's words expressed a truth that is visibly and vitally evident throughout the country. For there is scarcely a house that does not display the sublime picture of Our Lady of Guadalupe, and honour it daily as the centre of family devotion to the Mother of God. Its very presence transforms each home into a shrine in which Our Lady looks down on each member of the family with the same unearthly beauty and loving tenderness which once gazed on the enraptured face of Juan Diego. To all she utters those gentle and compelling words: "Am I not here who am your Mother?"

To mark the memorable occasion of his visit, Pope John Paul II composed the following prayer to Our Lady of Guadalupe:

"O Immaculate Virgin Mother of the true God and Mother of the Church! You, who from this place reveal your clemency and your pity to all those who ask for your protection; hear the prayer that we address to you with filial trust, and present it to your Son Jesus, our

Frank Smoczynski

An extraordinary view of the Shrine Square showing the New and Old Basilicas, plus a part of the Old Capuchin Convent on the far right. The serious tilt in the Old Basilica is graphically evident in this picture. Since Mexico City has been built on and around several lakes (all but one of which has been drained), many buildings in the area sink or tilt. Some can be jacked up; some must be torn down. The Old Basilica is sinking, which necessitated evacuation and building of the new edifice. The Old Basilica will be brought back to level by the expensive method of hydraulic jacking, after which it will become a museum.

Another view of the New Basilica of Guadalupe, finished in 1976 at a cost of some $70 million and capable of holding 10,000 people.

Frank Smoczynski

Translation of the Sacred Image from the Old Basilica to the New Basilica on October 12, 1976.

Above: Another view of the Shrine Square, showing the Old and New Basilicas with a typically large crowd of pilgrims.
Opposite: Two views showing the enshrinement of the Sacred Image in the New Basilica. A protective bullet-proof glass covers the Image itself.

Frank Smoczynski

Frank Smoczynski

An interior view of the New Basilica, looking across the foot of the sanctuary, on the right.

An aerial view of the Guadalupe complex and Tepeyac Hill, showing the New Basilica at the left, the Old Basilica center left, the Old Capuchin Convent at center right, *La Capilla de los Indios* (The Chapel of the Indians) at the near right, and the Baptistry at the far right. Immediately behind the Old Basilica is Tepeyac Hill, on top of which is a chapel called *El Cerrito*, built on the site of the first apparition.

Upper: Pilgrims visiting *El Cerrito* Chapel on Tepeyac Hill. This chapel is built on the site of the first apparition of Our Lady, which occurred on Saturday, 9 December 1531. The white building to the right is a Carmelite convent.

Lower: View from the foot of Tepeyac Hill with The Chapel of the Indians in the foreground and *El Cerrito* Chapel at the top of the hill in the background. Halfway up the hill can be seen the concrete replica of a mast and sails. (See opposite page for details.) The Original Hermitage (chapel) in which the Sacred Image was first enshrined is now the sacristy of The Chapel of the Indians.

Frank Smoczynski

Frank Smoczynski

Frank Smoczynski

Upper left: Concrete mast and sails on the side of Tepeyac Hill. In 1565 the ship *San Lucas* encountered a terrible storm at sea, which took away all the masts but one. The terrified sailors implored Our Lady of Guadalupe for help, promising that if they were spared, they would carry the remaining mast and sails in pilgrimage to her shrine. The storm died down and they gained harbor. True to their word, they brought the remaining mast and sails to Guadalupe to plant at her shrine as a memorial. The original has been replaced by one of concrete.

Upper right: Statue of Our Lady of Guadalupe on the ascent to Tepeyac Hill.

Lower: Statues of two angels plus a huge cross alongside *El Cerrito* Chapel on top of Tepeyac Hill.

Frank Smoczynski

View from Tepeyac Hill showing, in the foreground, the pathway ascending the hill plus the elaborate Baptistry; Mexico City is in the background.

sole Redeemer. Mother of mercy, Teacher of hidden and silent sacrifice, to you, who come to meet us sinners, we dedicate on this day all our being and all our love. We also dedicate to you our life, our work, our joys, our infirmities and our sorrows. Grant peace, justice and prosperity to our peoples, for we entrust to your care, Our Lady and our Mother, all that we have and all that we are. We wish to be entirely yours and to walk with you along the way of complete faithfulness to Jesus Christ in His Church: hold us always with your loving hand.

"Virgin of Guadalupe, Mother of the Americas, we pray to you for all the Bishops, that they may lead the faithful along the paths of intense Christian life, of love and humble service of God and souls. Contemplate this immense harvest, and intercede with the Lord that He may instil a hunger for holiness in the whole People of God, and grant abundant vocations of priests and religious, strong in the faith, and zealous dispensers of God's mysteries. Grant to our homes, the grace of loving and respecting life in its beginnings, with the same love with which you conceived in your womb the life of the Son of God.

"Blessed Virgin Mary, Mother of Fair Love, protect our families so that they may always be united, and bless the upbringing of our children. Our hope, look upon us with compassion, teach us to go continually to Jesus and, if we fall, help us to rise again, to return to Him, by means of the confession of our faults and sins in the Sacrament of Penance, which gives peace to the soul. We beg you to grant us a great love for all the holy Sacraments, which are, as it were, the signs that your Son left on earth. Thus, Most Holy Mother, with the peace of God in our conscience, with our hearts free from evil and hatred, we will be able to bring to all true joy and true peace, which come to us from your Son, our Lord Jesus Christ, who with God the Father and the Holy Spirit, lives and reigns for ever and ever. Amen."

Late in 1979 came a development of particular importance for English-speaking pilgrims at Guadalupe. Some years ago a centre had been established close to the shrine by Helen Behrens for all English-speaking visitors, but after her death, it was closed down. However, on 16 July 1979 the Queen of the Americas Guild meeting at the shrine of St. Elizabeth Seton, Emmitsburg, Maryland, resolved to try to establish another such centre at Guadalupe, to give pilgrims a deeper appreciation of the miracle and message of Guadalupe and of Our Lady's reassurance of her protection "to all those who dwell in these lands and to all mankind . . . who love me." The project was supported by eighty U.S. Bishops and a great number of prominent Catholics in that country. Early in December 1979, the Most Reverend Jerome Hastrich, President of the Guild, and John Haffert, Acting Secretary (and International Lay Delegate of the Blue Army of Our Lady of Fatima), flew to Mexico City with the intention of finding a suitable site and of forming a corporation there for the development and administration of the new centre.

A committee, which had previously been formed in Mexico City to prepare for the foundation of a new Centre for English-speaking pilgrims, assisted Bishop Hastrich and John Haffert in finding the most suitable location – a large property at 33, Via Allende. Next door was a Benedictine Convent of the Missionary Sisters of Our Lady of Guadalupe, with public accommodation for up to 300 people in three different auditoriums, a large chapel and dining room. The Sisters expressed their willingness to co-operate in the project and to extend their considerable facilities for the use of English-speaking pilgrims next door.

At a subsequent meeting in the city, the Mexican committee, with Bishop Hastrich and John Haffert, decided to name the building *Casa Regina* or *Queen of the Americas House* and to establish a corporation to organise and maintain it. The approval of the Abbot of the Basilica (Mgr. William Schulenburg) was secured and Cardinal Corripio of Mexico City expressed warm approval of the project and agreed to become a member of the temporary committee for the formation of the planned corporation. His Eminence later disclosed that Pope John Paul II had recently visited both him and Cardinal Miranda in the Mexican College, Rome, where, pausing before a painting of the sacred image, he said: "I feel drawn to this picture of Our Lady of Guadalupe because her face is full of kindness and simplicity . . . it calls me."

The establishment of this new centre will benefit British, Irish, Australian, New Zealand and many other English-speaking pilgrims who visit the shrine in ever-increasing numbers as the fame of the sacred image radiates through the world. One can be sure that Our Lady will welcome this new initiative to assist these distant visitors to acquire a deeper understanding of the significance of her portrait and her presence, epitomised in the words of the famous Jesuit poet, Father Abed: "Qua neque amabilius quidquam est ne pulchrius orbe." ("More beautiful or more lovable than it, there is nothing in this world.")

NOTES

1. *The Indian who saw Mary,* by Carmen Garcia.
2. *Handbook of Guadalupe,* p. 118.
3. *Juan Diego,* p. 13.
4. Address to Lay Apostles, 8 March 1966.
5. *Handbook of Guadalupe,* p. 20.

VII

THE VERDICT OF SCIENCE

BEFORE we examine the astonishing evidence to substantiate the supernatural origin of the sacred image, it is necessary to know something about the material on which it appears. The *tilma* was a regular Aztec outer garment for men, worn in front like a long apron and frequently looped up to serve as a carryall, or wrapped round the shoulders as a cloak. Several different styles of the garment were in use, designed for the various classes of Aztec society. The upper classes wore a *tilma* of cotton cloth which was knotted over the right shoulder, while the middle class, to which Juan Diego belonged, used a *tilma* made of ayate fibre, a coarse fabric derived from the threads of the maguey cactus plant. It was knotted over the left shoulder and had the colour of unbleached linen. The lower classes knotted the garment behind the neck, where it could serve for porter work.

The *tilma* of Juan Diego comprises two straight lengths of ayate fibre sewn together in the centre and woven so coarsely that when viewed close-up it appears to be almost transparent. During the sixteenth century the garment was cut down to the size of the image, which measures 66 inches by 41 inches. The figure of Our Lady is 56 inches tall and, as Coley Taylor noted, seems to increase in size as one draws back, due to some unknown property of the surface causing it to reflect the light that falls on it. The Virgin's head is inclined gracefully to the right, evading the centre seam which would otherwise disfigure her face, as if by some preconceived intuition. The eyes are downcast, but the pupils are clearly visible and, as we have observed, seemingly vibrant with life. The overall impression of her features is one of incomparable tenderness and supernatural lovingness, which mere words are powerless to portray.

To date, the sublime picture has consistently defied exact reproduction, whether by brush or camera. Copies, however meticulously executed, fail to convey the ineffable delicacy of the Virgin's expression and the exquisite delineation of her eyes and

THE VERDICT OF SCIENCE

THE VERDICT OF SCIENCE

lips. Nor, of course, can they reproduce the mysterious changing colours observed in the image, which will be discussed later. "The greatest masters of the art of painting," wrote Professor Tanco Becerra in 1666, "confess . . . that a beauty of countenance so modestly joyful is humanly inimitable." And a century later, the great Mexican painter Ibarra wrote: "No painter has ever been found capable of sketching or copying Our Lady of Guadalupe . . . Its singular uniqueness proves the picture to be the invention, not of a human artist, but of the Almighty."[1]

Considerable efforts have been made during the past few decades to produce an exact photographic reproduction of the sacred image with the aid of sophisticated camera equipment and lighting techniques. But the best results achieved have only been distortions by comparison with the matchless beauty of the glowing original. The most that can be said of the millions of copies in existence is that they remind one of the original. By general assent, the least imperfect copy is the one at the U.S. National Shrine of Our Lady of the Americas at Allentown, Pennsylvania.

We have already noted that the lifespan of the ayate fibre is approximately twenty years. Yet after four hundred and fifty years, the *tilma* still shows not the slightest sign of decay. Its colours remain as vivid and fresh as when they first materialised before Bishop Zumárraga's astounded gaze. And this despite the fact that for over a century the sacred image hung unprotected even by glass in a damp, open-windowed chapel the size of an average living-room, where it was directly exposed to ceaseless smoke and incense, burnt perfumes and the myriads of votive candles flickering beneath it.

The emissions of burning wax in particular are notoriously destructive, since they include corrosive hydrocarbons, ionisations and soot. The cumulative pollution in such a confined space should have blackened the picture beyond recognition. One has only to recall the smoke-darkened rock of the Lourdes' grotto, which is wide open to the wind, to appreciate the rigours of pollution to which the sacred image was subjected during those early years. Yet still it retained its pristine beauty and enchanting freshness to the wonderment of all.

Professor Philip Callahan, a biophysicist at the University of Florida who studied the celestial picture in 1979, stated in his report that he once measured over six hundred microwatts of near ultra-violet light from a single votive candle. Multiply this by a factor of hundreds of thousands or more and we have an intolerable environment for any painting. "Excess ultra-violet light," he wrote, "quickly fades most colour pigments, whether organic or inorganic, especially blues." But the sacred image appears to be indestructible, as if immune from the most damaging effects of human ill-treatment.

During the years when it hung unprotected in the damp stone chapel at Tepeyac for example, it was touched by literally millions of loving hands and lips – the same unwearyingly persistent contact of veneration which has worn smooth the rock of the Lourdes grotto. Men touched it with their swords; women with their ornaments. Others, moved by a transport of fervour, embraced it, grasping the delicate material with their hands and caressing it with passionate devotion as if it were a living thing. Countless sick persons applied the *tilma* to their diseased or disabled bodies, and many of the over-zealous stealthily removed threads from the garment for priceless relics. Even after the sacred image had been mounted behind a protective glass screen, the latter had to be removed at frequent intervals to satisfy the incessant pleading of thousands of ardent devotees who yearned to touch it just once more, or to kiss the beautiful face. In 1753, Miguel Cabrera recorded that on one occasion, he saw the *tilma* touched with various objects five hundred times in the space of two hours.

The extraordinary fragility of the *tilma* is immediately apparent from the single thin cotton thread down the centre which holds the two pieces of ayate together. "This fragile thread," declared Cabrera, "resists and, for more than two centuries, has resisted the natural force of gravity and the weight of the two pieces which it unites and which are themselves made of much heavier and coarser stuff."[2]

The environment at Tepeyac was, and still is, far from ideal for the preservation of almost any work of art. The area is exposed to winds which are frequently laden with moisture or dust. The undrained marshes which surrounded Mexico City for centuries exuded a corrosive vapour which ate into anything from fabrics to solid stonework and cement. "That this universally penetrating, deleterious influence should have been withstood by the frail *tilma* alone", observed Fr. Lee, "is a cause of legitimate admiration. And the climax of this wonder is the preservation of the delicate colours in all their rich freshness."[3]

These enduring attributes of the sacred image have caused more than one rationalist to bow before the supernatural evidence confronting him. In 1976 for instance, an agnostic architect named Ramirez Vasquez, who was entrusted with the design of the new basilica, requested permission to study the sacred image. He examined it so thoroughly that he became a Catholic.

Yet another factor pointing to the supernatural origin of the sacred image has been its inexplicable preservation during the several disasters that have threatened it over the centuries. In 1791 for example, a workman cleaning the gold and silver frame enclosing the picture, accidentally spilt a bottle of nitric acid across the image. Instead of destroying the delicate fabric, the acid, to the workman's dumbfounded relief, left a barely discernible watermark on the material.

An even more dramatic protection was accorded to the sacred image during the violent persecution of the Church in Mexico in the 1920s under the despotic rule of Plutarco Calles. Churches were closed and many priests and nuns were martyred, including the saintly Father Miguel Pro, who fell before a firing-squad crying: "Long live Christ the King!" But the regime dared not close the beloved shrine of Our Lady of Guadalupe for fear of provoking an incalculable backlash. Instead, they resorted to the diabolical strategem of trying to tear out the heart of the Mexican peoples' faith. On 14 November 1921, a powerful time bomb was concealed in a large vase of flowers and placed immediately under the sacred image. At 10.30 a.m., during High Mass, the bomb exploded with a shattering roar, ripping out jagged chunks of marble and masonry from the sanctuary and shivering to fragments the magnificent stained glass windows of the Basilica. A heavy iron cross on the devastated altar was twisted like modelling clay. But when the cloud of smoke and dust lifted, gasps of amazement and relief rose from the stunned celebrants and congregation, none of whom, astonishingly, was seriously injured. The priceless image was completely unscathed, and the thin protective glass covering was not even cracked, as if an invisible arm had warded off the monstrous blow.

After the persecution ceased, the celestial portrait was mounted behind bullet-proof glass and a special Chapel of Reparation to the Blessed Sacrament was opened to atone for this and other outrages perpetrated during the Calles regime. The twisted iron cross was displayed in a glass cabinet nearby to remind pilgrims of the amazing protection accorded to the sacred image during that searing blast.

"Our Lady is loved very much at the Basilica of Guadalupe," says Henry F. Unger, "but her Son is definitely not forgotten. The continuing stream of Mexicans to the Chapel of Reparation attests to this fact. From the evil perpetrated in the huge Basilica of Mexico

Frank Smoczynski

Dr. Charles Wahlig

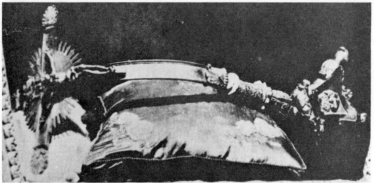

Dr. Charles Wahlig

Upper left: A beautiful monument in white Carrara marble depicting Juan Diego before Bishop Zumarraga at the moment of the Miracle of the Sacred Image. The Mexican people presented this monument to Pope Pius XII in 1939, and he had it erected in the Vatican Gardens, where, it is claimed, he went every day to pray.

Upper right: A colossal statue of Our Lady of Guadalupe erected in 1947 on the peak of Mt. Maggiorasca, the highest mountain (5,824 ft.) in the vicinity of Aveto, Italy. The statue now stands atop a lovely monument and is Italy's greatest shrine of Guadalupe.

Lower: The heavy bronze altar crucifix which formerly stood above the main altar of the Old Basilica of Guadalupe. On 14 November 1921 this crucifix was bent by a powerful time bomb placed by saboteurs in a vase of flowers immediately beneath the Sacred Image. Though the bomb shattered the windows and bent this crucifix, it did not even crack the protective glass over the Image.

City, when Our Lady stayed the principal effects of an evil-doer's time bomb, a glorious chapel of daily reparation has evolved to bring consolation to the Eucharistic Lord near the spot where Juan Diego first met the Blessed Mother."[4]

Over the centuries, the sacred image has been subjected to a variety of detailed examinations and close studies by experts on art and by scientists to determine whether there could be any possible natural explanation for its existence. But every investigation to date, whether by microscope, infra-red radiation or computer-enhanced photography, has pointed to its supernatural origin. Infra-red radiation photography, as we shall see, is particularly revealing since it can unmask brush strokes, detect painting corrections, and, of particular importance, expose the existence of a preliminary drawing underneath, an essential prerequisite for nearly all paintings.

In 1936 a German professor living in Mexico, Fritz Hahn, was invited by his government to attend the Olympic Games in Berlin that year. Just before he left for Europe, he was given two fibres from the sacred image, one red and one yellow, by Dr. Ernesto Pallanes, who had received them from the Bishop of Saltillo, who in turn had been given them by Don Feliciano Echavarria, priest of the Basilica, for the Bishop's reliquary. Together with the two fibres, Professor Hahn took a letter of recommendation from Professor Marcelino Junco, retired professor of organic chemistry at the National University of Mexico, to the German Nobel Prize winner in chemistry, Richard Kuhn, director of the chemistry department at the Kaiser Wilhelm Institution in Heidelberg. Kuhn examined the fibres with his accustomed thoroughness and then made an unbelieveable announcement. There was no colouring of any kind in the fibres. The materials used to produce what resembled colours were unknown to science, being neither animal, vegetable nor mineral dyes. The use of synthetic colouring was ruled out since that was developed three centuries *after* the creation of the sacred image.

The hypothesis that the sacred image is a painting was further discredited in 1946 when a microscope examination revealed that there were no brush strokes. Nor was there any sign of the usual artist's signature in the bottom corner of the picture. In 1954 and again in 1966, Mexican Professor Francisco Camps Ribera undertook an exhaustive study of the sacred image and came to the same conclusion. If, then, the picture was not a painting, what was it? Its material composition had to be something definable since it was observable and indeed tangible. But if it was of supernatural origin, how could this be equated with the material world, in terms of physical science?

As far back as 1929, a professional photographer named Alfonso Gonzales enalrged a photograph of the sacred image several times and was amazed to discover what appeared to be a human face in the eyes of Our Lady. His findings were kept confidential, pending further investigation, but the implications of his discovery never really made any impression on the authorities and the matter was eventually shelved and then forgotten.

On 29 May 1951, a draughtsman named J. Carlos Salinas Chavaz was examining a large photograph of the face of the sacred image under a powerful magnifying glass. As the lens moved across the pupil of the right eye, he was suddenly astonished to see the features and bust of a bearded man. The phenomenon prompted the Archbishop of Mexico City, Luis Marie Martinez, to set up a special investigating commission. The discovery was confirmed and on 11 December 1955 it was made public, together with the dramatic disclosure that the human face in the eye of Our Lady had been positively identified from a contemporary painting as that of Juan Diego.

The following July, two occulists, Drs. Javier Torroello Buene and Rafael Torifa Lavoignet, examined the eyes of the sacred image close up, initially without a magnifying glass. "Certain details surprised me, especially the light reflections," Dr. Lavoignet told Brother Bruno Bonnet-Eymard later. The doctor then scrutinised the eyes through a powerful magnifying glass. "I did know that a human bust had been discovered in the eyes of the Guadulupa," he confessed to Brother Bruno. "I observed with the greatest attention and indeed, I noticed that a human bust is to be seen in the cornea of both eyes. I looked first in the right eye and then in the left. Surprised, I thought it was necessary to examine the fact by the means of scientific procedures."

On 23 July 1956, Dr. Lavoignet undertook a meticulous examination of the eyes with an ophthalmoscope, "In the cornea of the eyes," he told Brother Bruno, "a human bust can be seen. The distortion and place of the optical image are indentical with what is produced in a normal eye. When the light of the ophthalmoscope is directed onto the pupil of a human eye, a light reflection is seen to shine on its outer circle. By following this reflection and by suitably changing the lenses of the ophthalmoscope, it is possible to obtain the image at the back of the eye. By directing the ophthalmoscope light onto the pupil of the eye of the Image of the Virgin, the same light reflection appears. As a consequence of this reflection, the pupil lights up in a diffused manner, giving the impression of hollow relief . . . This reflection is impossible to obtain on a flat surface and one, moreover, that is opaque as is this picture. I then examined by means of the ophthalmoscope the eyes of various paintings, both in oils and water colour and those of photographs. On none of them, all of different people, was the least reflection to be seen, whereas the eyes of the Blessed Virgin of Guadalupe give the impression of life."

In continuing this fascinating account, we can do no better than quote Brother Bruno's own words: "It all looks as though a light ray were entering a cavity, filling out a volumetric ocular globe, radiating from within a diffuse light. I did the experiment myself with an ophthalmoscope. The bronze, hazel-coloured eye of the Blessed Virgin lights up, and on the surface there shines quite distinctly the silhouette of a human bust. The head is turned threequarters towards the Virgin's right and slightly bent forward; the chest is framed and lengthened by a movement of the arms going forward as though to show something. It all happened as though, at the moment of the Image being impressed, a man who was facing the Blessed Virgin, and reflected in the cornea of her eye, had himself been *photographed* in this indirect way.

"There is more," he continued. "The image of this bust shows a distortion in exact conformity with the laws of such a reflection *in vivo*." Another surgeon, Doctor Javier Torroella Bueno, noticed it: "If we take a square piece of paper and place it in front of the eye," he told Brother Bruno in 1979, "we realise that the cornea is not flat (nor is it spherical) for a distortion of the image is produced which is a function of the place of the cornea, where it is reflected." Furthermore, if the paper is moved to a certain distance, it is also reflected "in the counterlateral corner of the other eye, that is to say, if an image is reflected in the temporal region of the right eye, it will be reflected in the nasal region of the left eye." The experiment is verified in our Image, in inverse conditions: the silhouette of the same bearded man is reflected in the nasal region of the right eye and also appears in the temporal corner of the left eye. The distortion of the reflected image is even more striking, for it is in perfect obedience to the laws of curvature of the cornea."

Predictably, the news had a stunning impact in Mexico. The mystery was there for all who took the trouble to investigate it. The distortion and dissymmetry of the two images conformed exactly with the laws of optics. In consequence, this obviated any explanation of the viewer being the victim of subjective impression, whether accidentally or because of the textile. It was as if Juan

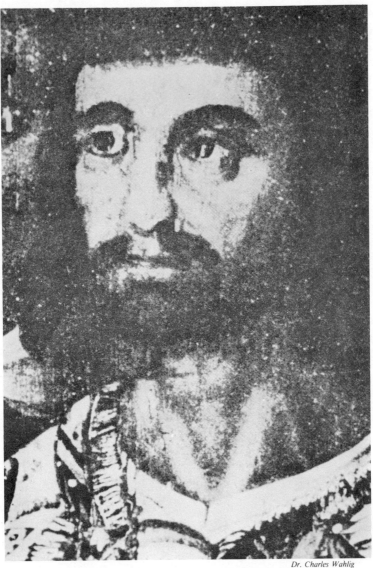

Dr. Charles Wahlig

Opposite: An enlarged view of the right eye of the Sacred Image of Our Lady of Guadalupe. To the right of the iris one can see the face and shoulders of a man. Further enlargement shows what appear to be two other faces.

Above: An enlarged picture of Juan Diego from an early painting. This painting is said to be the best likeness we have of Juan Diego. There is a striking similarity between the image in the Virgin's eye and the painting above.

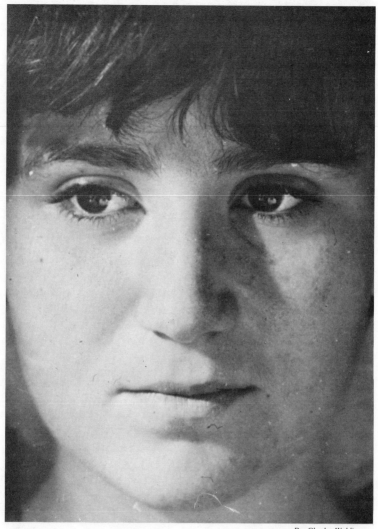

Dr. Charles Wahlig

Above: Dr. Charles Wahlig, an optometrist and one of the leading experts on Guadalupe, performed an experiment to illustrate the mirror principle of the human eye. His daughter Mary poses for the above photo while Dr. Wahlig, his wife and his daughter Carol stand opposite her.

Opposite: Enlargements of the right eye (above) and left eye (below) reveal the images of the three people who stand opposite from the subject. This same effect, typical of photographs, is found in the eyes of Our Lady of Guadalupe. Paintings do not possess this type of reflection.

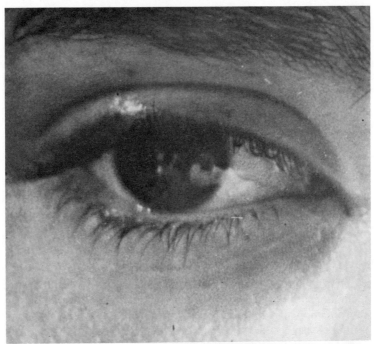

Dr. Charles Wahlig

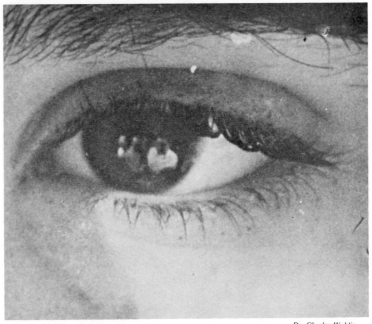

Dr. Charles Wahlig

Diego's *tilma* had been an exposed colour film which had photographed the Virgin (albeit invisible to the human eye) at the very moment when he was reflected in her eyes – an incredible fact which has lain concealed for over four hundred years and has at last been revealed and confirmed by modern science!

These extraordinary findings were followed in 1962 by a further exciting discovery. Dr. C. Wahlig, O.D., and his wife Isabelle, an optician, examined a photograph of the sacred image enlarged twenty-five times and found not only two more faces reflected in the eyes, but by applying the law of reflections in convex mirrors, they succeeded in reconstructing the exact circumstances under which the celestial portrait was created.

"The cornea functions as a convex mirror with a radius of about 7.5 mm, varying slightly from person to person," explained Dr. Wahlig in a report dated September 1963. "Our son-in-law, Edward Gebhardt, has a great deal of experience with photography techniques and suggested two possible ways of making the reproduction. The first was to photograph the eye at short range and obtain clearly visible reflections of people situated in front of the eye. The second method was to photograph a person at a distance of several feet, next enlarge the photograph until the eye filled the picture, then study the reflections of the people confronting the person whose eye was being photographed. We decided that the first pictures should be taken using the first method." He continued: "With a camera especially constructed for taking close-up photographs, we took pictures of our family arranged similarly to the way we believe the original scene existed as portrayed in Our Lady's eye. Our daughter Mary posed as Our Lady, and it is her eye which is photographed in the pictures. My wife, myself and our daughter Carol took positions in front of Mary, and our reflections appear in the cornea of her eye, as can be seen in the accompanying photographs . . .

"At the time when Juan Diego presented the bishop with the flowers, Our Lady was actually present in the room, but chose to remain invisible. Instead, in order to give a visible, lasting indication of her presence, she chose to imprint upon Juan Diego's blanket an authentic picture of herself as she stood there watching the scene. The picture is complete in every detail, even to the reflections in her eye of Juan Diego and two other people standing near him and of someone apparently looking over his shoulder. It seems from the posture of Juan Diego and the other two that they were not aware of Our Lady's presence. The two appear to be looking at Juan Diego and he, we may assume, is looking at the bishop."

It is important to note that corneal eye reflections had not been given scientific verification until Baron Von Helmholtz validated them in a great treatise on the eye published in the 1880s.[5] Since it was not possible to capture them until the invention of the camera, we are presented with a scientifically inexplicable phenomenon, namely, who could have known about them and used them in 1531?

Dr. Wahlig's report continued: "Much has been said as to why the original enlargements made from the picture of Our Lady were made of the right eye only. While the image formation of an individual should be reflected equally in both eyes, there could be, and actually are physical circumstances which could prevent them from being exactly alike . . . There would be even greater differences in the reflections in the two eyes in the sacred image due to the texture of the cloth, such as abberrations in the weave and imperfections in the cloth itself. For practical reasons, the reflections in the right eye were used, being more well defined than those in her left eye."[6]

Dr. Wahlig acknowleged the collaboration of an impressive number of distinguished specialists in this technically difficult experiment. Among them were Dr. Francis T. Avignone, a practicing optometrist and formerly a lecturer in practical optics and optometry at Columbia University; Mr. Edward Gebhardt, a television engineer with the National Broadcasting Company, who took the photographs; Dr. Michael Wahlig, Ph.D. (his son); Dr. Alexander Wahlig, M.D. (his brother and an eye surgeon); the late Dr. H. G. Noyes, M.D., opthalmologist and a former lecturer in optical sciences at Columbia University, New York; Dr. Glen Fry, Ph.D., in charge of optical developments for the U.S. Government during World War II; Dr. Italo Mannelli, Professor of physics and head of the department in the University of Pisa, Italy; and Dr. Wahlig's wife, a B.A. and as we have noted, an experienced optician.

Shortly after these discoveries had been made, the second figure reflected in Our Lady's eyes was tentatively identified as Juan Gonzales, the interpreter, who had been standing beside Juan Diego when he unfolded his *tilma* in front of Bishop Zumárraga. This identification was made possible by the discovery in 1960 of a long-lost painting of the miracle of the dead man being restored to life. The picture, which had been executed about 1533 by three artists who were personally familiar with the leading characters of the Guadalupe story and who were therefore able to delineate an accurate likeness of them, was discovered behind the altar of the old 1622 church when it was restored in 1960.

The discovery was important in more ways than one, since there had been a theory circulating in Mexico that the three images in Our Lady's eyes were all of Juan Diego, the third image being inverted in compliance with the Purkenje-Sanson law of optic physiology. That the second image in Our Lady's right eye bears a strong resemblance to Juan Gonzales is immediately clear when examined under a powerful glass. The third image, although very indistinct, is strongly reminiscent of the features of Bishop Ramirez y Fuenleal who was known for certain to have been in the room at the time.[7]

"The coming to light of the existence of this painting at that particular time took on a special significance," stated Dr. Wahlig. "It was as though it were part of a plan to represent the portrait of Our Lady to all living in our era as being a scientifically validated supernatural phenomenon. When the studies of the reflections in Our Lady's eyes in her picture were being pursued in 1962, the discovery of the 1533 painting two years earlier provided a reliable medium for identification . . ."

Dr. Wahlig confirmed that the third image "shows a strong resemblance" to Bishop Ramirez y Fuenleal, who had just been appointed general administrator of Mexico. "This disclosure complements the other related discoveries of a scientific nature," concluded Dr. Wahlig, "which confirm in striking ways the word of the persons who lived hundreds of years ago (i.e. the historians), that the sacred image is truly a portrait from heaven."[8]

In a letter to the present writer dated 6 December 1979, Dr. Wahlig explained: "We derived a measure of satisfaction from the painting by Miguel Cabrera, Mexico's greatest colonial painter (of the scene when the image was created), which shows the three persons in about the same positions as they are reflected in Our Lady's eyes. This picture was painted about 1750, which shows there must have been a strong tradition that those were the circumstances existing at the moment of the creation of the sacred image."

The painting referred to is presently hanging in the old Basilica of Guadalupe and shows Bishop Zumárraga facing Juan Diego, Juan Gonzales and Bishop Fuenleal. Our Lady must therefore have been present immediately behind Bishop Zumárraga and facing the three men standing before him, whose images would be reflected in her eyes – an amazing relevation reserved by Providence for discovery by science in an unbelieving age, four centuries later. The scientific demonstration of the eye images received additional support in 1963 when members of the management of Kodak de Mexico, S.A., announced that the sacred image was essentially photographic in character. It only remained for scientists to determine if it was possible to demonstrate physically the supernatural origin of the sacred image.

A step in this direction was taken in May 1979 when two high-ranking American scientists, Professor Philip Callahan of the University of Florida and Professor Jody Smith of Pensacola, Florida, spurred by recent investigations into the Shroud of Turin, took some sixty photographs of the sacred image, many in infra-red radiation, to determine if there was a preliminary artist's drawing under the picture. Other photographs were to be computer-enhanced and studied for clues as to the image's origin. "I'm interested in doing what William James said a hundred years ago – to bring together religion and science," stated Professor Smith at the outset. "In our culture, we live lives that are too compartmentalised."

Professor Callahan was eminently qualified for the task. A prolific writer of science books, he was also an experienced painter, photographer and an authority in the field of infra-red radiation, especially in the study of its effects on molecules. Professor Jody Smith, a Methodist, who had earlier received permission to study the sacred image, decided that Professor Callahan was the ideal scientist to assist him in the exacting investigation.

Infra-red photography is the latest and most comprehensive method of studying old paintings and documents to determine their historical derivation, method of composition and validity. Since pigments vary in their manner of transmitting and reflecting infra-red light, this system of photography is able to unmask overpaintings and alterations. It has become a standard scientific tool in the field of art research. The penetrating wavelengths of infra-red light can see through a varnish coating or surface layer of dirt, expose the original painting beneath it and even determine the nature of the sizing below that, providing the layer of size is not too thick. "No study of a work of art can be considered complete," stated Professor Callahan in his subsequent report, "until the techniques of infra-red photography have been utilised. And certainly no valid scientific study is complete without such an analysis."

The tests were conducted on the *tilma* itself on 7 May 1979 from 9 p.m. till midnight, in the presence of a bishop, a policeman and a number of workmen. "We may never be able to understand the cloak," Professor Jody Smith admitted beforehand, "but the way to try is to do what research we can." The results of their meticulous investigation are summarised as follows:

The picture dating from 1531 cannot be explained by science. Its colour rendering, and the preservation of its brightness over the centuries are inexplicable. There is definitely no under-drawing, no sizing and no protective over-varnish present on the image. Without sizing, the *tilma* should have rotted centuries ago, and without protective varnishing, the picture should have been ruined long ago by prolonged exposure to candle smoke and other pollutants, as was mentioned earlier. Under high magnification, the image shows no detectable sign of fading or cracking – an inexplicable occurrence after 450 years of existence. Powerful lenses also revealed the astonishing fact that the coarse weave of the *tilma* had been deliberately utilised in a precise manner to give depth to the face of the image. "It may seem strange for a scientist to say this," concluded Professor Callahan, "but as far as I am concerned, the original picture is miraculous."

The face of the Virgin, he acknowledges, is a masterpiece of artistic expression. Its subtlety of appearance and simplicity of design, hue and colouring put it in a unique class of its own. The infra-red close-up pictures show no brushmarks and the absence of sizing is patent in the many unfilled spaces visible in the fabric. Such a phenomenon is "fantastic", Professor Callahan concluded.

The scientists agreed that the sublime face of the Virgin exhibits an almost lifelike appearance, especially in the area around the mouth, where a coarse fibre elevated above the wave perfectly follows the ridge at the top of the lip, imparting a three-dimensional aspect. Similar effects occur below the left cheek and to the right of and below the right eye. Professor Callahan thought it impossible that any human painter could have selected a *tilma* with the imperfections of its weave so precisely positioned as to accentuate the shadows and highlights, in order to convey such realism.

The two scientists were particularly impressed by the use of the rough fabric to cause light diffraction. Viewed close-up, the face and hands are a grey-white colour which gradually becomes olive as one backs away – an impossible accomplishment for any human painter. "The same effect is found in nature," Professor Callahan observed, "when colours change under different angles, such as with bird feathers, butterfly scales, and on the elytra of brightly coloured beetles."

The pink robe and especially the blue mantle of the Virgin merited closer study, since all the known pigments that could have been used to produce them would have faded long ago, and the torrid Mexican summers would only have accelerated this process. Yet the colouring remains as brilliant and fresh as if it has just been laid on. The pink colouring of the robe was found to be transparent to infra-red light, and this highlighted another mystery. Most pink pigments are opaque to infra-red light but there is no trace in the image of the few that are not.

For all the value of his study, Professor Callahan seems to have faltered by claiming that the areas which were touched up in the past were actually painted additions made to the image a century after its creation. For, as the Lepanto copy of the sacred image proves, this theory is untenable. Meticulous visual inspections of the picture by a number of experts in the recent past, especially that undertaken by Dr. Charles J. Wahlig, O.D., on the night on 5 September 1975, clearly indicate that the areas claimed by Professor Callahan to be painted additions to the original, were merely painted overlays. Thus an original white sunburst can be seen under the flaking gold leaf of the rays, and an original moon, much smaller in size, is just visible under the present crescent, which was applied with silver paint, but which has since turned black, and so on.

The face and hands were painted darker. The latter were shortened, apparently to make Our Lady appear more Mexican, and traces of a lighter colour to the skin underneath can just be seen with a magnifying glass. Even the left eye was touched up, certainly after 1923, for a careful examination of photographs taken in that year show three eye reflections as clearly as those in the right eye. Apparently the partial obscuring of these images in the left eye was due to carelessness on the part of the painter when outlining the lid margins.

"Studying the image," Professor Callahan concluded, "was the most moving experience of my life. Just getting that close, I got the same strange feeling that others did who worked on the Shroud of Turin." He added, "I believe in logical explanations up to a point. But there is no logical explanation for life. You can break life down into atoms, but what comes after that? Even Einstein said God."

As we end this account of the story of Guadalupe, one cannot help asking what is the significance of the sacred image for our present-day world, saturated with sin and threatened with nuclear war? Why has the brief life-span of the *tilma's* ayate fabric been prolonged inexplicably for four hundred and fifty years? Why has the delicate material withstood the stain of millions of hands and candles, where even the hard rock of the Lourdes' grotto has had to yield? Why did the fiery bite of nitric acid fail to shrivel the frailest of fabrics? And above all, why did a Divine hand interpose itself in

1921 between the helpless *tilma* and the searing blast of a powerful bomb which had been exploded just beneath it?

If the answer is simply that Our Lady wished her sacred image to be perpetuated among the peoples of the Western Hemisphere, we must again ask why. Has she some predestined purpose for the Americas, perhaps assuring them of their ultimate protection and safety, as Pope Pius XII believed?

We know that today the devil is engaged in a last great onslaught with the Woman who is destined to crush his head. Her coming triumph was announced on 13 July 1917 at Fatima: "In the end, my Immaculate Heart will triumph." But before that consummation so devoutly to be wished, she warned that the enemy would intensify his attack as he sees his time running short. On all sides there is evidence of the ferocious war being waged by the powers of Hell against the Woman and her children. One need only remember the savage attack on Michelangelo's beautiful *Pieta* by a man crying, "I am the devil," or the blasphemous outrage against Our Lady of Guadalupe herself a few months earlier, in 1972, when an American film director deliberately deceived the Abbot of the shrine as to his true intention, and made his troupe of actors and actresses enact diabolical rituals and pornographic sequences *inside the Sanctuary*. Such heinous sacrileges are symptomatic of the terrifying power of Satan. "We are all under an obscure domination" warned Pope Paul VI in his November 1972 address on the spread of doctrinal error, devil worship and the occult. "It is that of Satan, the Prince of this world, the Number One enemy."

There is a striking parellel between our own age and that of the Aztec civilisation immediately before the apparitions of 1531. Now as then, society is dominated by godlessness, pagan excesses and immorality. Countless innocents today are sacrificed alive on the altars of abortion. False deities abound everywhere. Aztec polygamy and depravity are more than matched by today's universal moral collapse. A decisive collision seems inevitable and imminent, as it was in 1531.

But all is not lost. The darkest hour will inevitably melt away in the radiant dawn of Our Lady's triumph over the serpent. A tiny minority are complying with the crucial Fatima message of 1917 and, through unwearying prayer and personal sacrifice – such as all-night vigils of reparation – strive to redress the fearful imbalance created by so much deliberate evil. As in 1531, when only a handful of clerics were praying for deliverance, we can surely trust that, if the faithful few of today persevere and multiply their ranks, Our

Frank Smoczynski

Pope John Paul II blessing the assembly gathered in the Shrine Square during his visit to Guadalupe on 27 January 1979 on his way to the Latin American Bishops' Conference at Puebla. Behind the Holy Father stands a replica of the Sacred Image made of flowers. The Pope stands on the balcony of the New Basilica after having celebrated Mass there. Pope John Paul II is the only pontiff who has visited Guadalupe.

Lady will intervene again and overwhelm the powers of darkness with the brightness of her presence.

This, perhaps, is the ultimate significance of the sacred image in Mexico City today. Four hundred and fifty years ago, a tangible pledge of hope was left to us by the Mother of Christ, who is our Mother also, if we profess to be truly her Son's brethren. She gave us this pledge in order to sustain us during the world-wide rationalist revolt against God which has arisen over the past few centuries, and is now reaching its terrible climax. From the centre of the American continent, there blazes a beacon of reassurance in a nightmarish world, a star above the storm, a supernatural Statue of Liberty holding up the Light of the World – the Truth that will set men really free – and proclaiming to the people who walk in darkness a wondrous message of thrilling hope:

"I am your merciful Mother, the Mother of all who live united in this land, and of all mankind, of all those who love me, of those who cry to me, of those who have confidence in me. Here I will hear their weeping and their sorrows, and will remedy and alleviate their sufferings, necessities and misfortunes . . . Do not be troubled or weighed down with grief. Do not fear any illness or vexation, anxiety or pain. Am I not here who am your Mother? Are you not under my shadow and protection? Am I not your fountain of life? Are you not in the folds of my mantle? In the crossing of my arms? Is there anything else you need?"

NOTES

1. *Maravilla Americana,* p. 10.
2. *Ibid,* p. 2.
3. *Our Lady of Guadalupe,* p. 165.
4. *A Handbook on Guadalupe,* p. 119.
5. *A Treatise on Physiological Optics.*
6. The full report of Dr. Wahlig appears as an appendix in his superb book, *Juan Diego.*
7. It needs to be stressed that Purkenje-Sanson images cannot be photographed.
8. cf. *A Handbook on Guadalupe,* p. 63.

CHRONOLOGICAL SUMMARY OF EVENTS

1531   December 9th: First and Second apparitions of the Blessed Virgin to Juan Diego at Tepeyac.

1531   December 10th: Third apparition of the Blessed Virgin to Juan Diego at Tepeyac.

1531   December 12th: Fourth apparition at Tepeyac; creation of the miraculous image in the presence of Bishop Zumárraga and apparition of Our Lady to Juan Bernardino in Tolpetlac, who is cured of a fatal sickness.

1531   December: The image is exposed in the Bishop's private chapel where it is venerated by thousands of Aztecs. Completion of the first small sanctuary at Tepeyac.

1531   December 26th: Triumphant procession bears the sacred image from Mexico City to Tepeyac. A Mexican, accidentally killed by an arrow, is restored to life before the image.

1533   Larger chapel, known as the *Second Hermitage,* is constructed at Tepeyac to house the sacred image.

1539   Conversion of Mexico largely completed; 8,000,000 Aztecs embrace the Catholic Faith as a direct result of the creation of the sacred image.

1544   May 15th: Death of Juan Bernardino, aged 84, at Tolpetlac.

1544   Pilgrimage of children to Tepeyac immediately results in the cessation of a deadly plague that had killed 12,000 in Mexico City alone.

1545   Earliest written account of the apparitions by Don Antonio Valeriano, the *Nican Mopohua*.

1548   Death of Juan Diego, aged 74, at Tepeyac.

1556   The third hermitage is built at Tepeyac by D. Alonso de Montufar, O.P., second Archbishop of Mexico.

1557   The Archbishop of Mexico canonically establishes the truth of the apparitions.

1570   An inventory of the Archbishopric of Mexico is sent to Phillip II of Spain by D. Alonso de Montufar O.P., including the hermitage chapel at Tepeyac. A painting of the sacred image sent to the king at the same time was to play a significant part in the Battle of Lepanto.

1629   A disastrous flood in Mexico City drowns 30,000 inhabitants. The sacred image is conveyed to the city by a procession of boats and remains in the cathedral until the waters abate.

1634   May 14th: The sacred image returns to Tepeyac in a vast procession of thanksgiving to mark the ending of the flood.

1709   April: Solemn dedication of the first Basilica of Our Lady of Guadalupe at Tepeyac.

1736   Mexico is stricken by a plague of typhus which claims some 700,000 lives.

1737   April 27th: The plague ceases as Our Lady of Guadalupe is proclaimed Patroness of the country. December 12th is proclaimed a holy day and civil holiday.

1754   April 24th: In Rome, the Sacred Congregation of Rites issues a decree approving an Office and Mass for Our Lady of Guadalupe.

1754   April 25th: Pope Benedict XIV issues a Bull approving Our Lady of Guadalupe as Patroness of Mexico and quotes Psalm 147: He hath not done in like manner to every nation.

1756   First serious examination of the sacred image by the celebrated painter Miguel Cabrera and other artists, who declare it would be impossible to reproduce it perfectly.

1777   Work commences on the Chapel of the Well at Tepeyac, situated on the eastern side of the plaza.

1791   The sacred image is miraculously preserved from destruction when nitric acid, used to clean the gold and silver frame, is accidentally spilled across the delicate fabric of the picture, leaving nothing more than a watermark.

1802   Chapel erected at Cuauhtitlan, birthplace of Juan Diego.

1821   At the end of the Mexican War of Independence, Emperor Augustin de Iturbide of the new nation solemnly confides the country to the care of Our Lady of Guadalupe.

1890   Renovation of the Basilica of Our Lady of Guadalupe.

1894   Pope Leo XIII approves new Office and Mass of Our Lady of Guadalupe.

1895   October 12th: First crowning of the sacred image authorised by Pope Leo XIII.

1910   August 24th: Our Lady of Guadalupe proclaimed Patroness of Latin America by Pope Pius X.

1921   November 14th. Further miraculous preservation of the sacred image when a bomb, exploded beneath it by anti-religious Government agents, did not even crack its glass cover.

1929   Reflected image of a man seen in the eyes of the image by Alfonso Marcué González. His discovery remains unpublished until 1960, on the advice of the sanctuary authorities.

1933   December 12th: Solemn Pontifical Mass in St. Peter's, Rome, in presence of Pope Pius XI who repeats Pope St. Pius X's proclamation of Our Lady of Guadalupe as Patroness of Latin America.

1945   October 12th: Pope Pius XII commemorates the 50th anniversary of the first crowning of the sacred image in a radio address to the people of Mexico.

1946   Investigations show that the portrait of Our Lady is devoid of brush strokes, indicating that it could not have been painted.

1951   Carlos Salinas examines the sacred image and notes the images in the eyes.

1955   A young boy in Tolpetlac discovers the stone cross that marked the spot where Juan Diego found his dying uncle.

1955   December 11th: Radio announcement confirms that the image of a man seen in the eyes of the portrait is definitely that of Juan Diego.

1962   Dr. and Mrs. Charles J. Wahlig, O.D., of New York discover two more reflected images in the eyes of the portrait after studying a photograph of the face of the portrait enlarged twenty-five times. Dr. Wahlig proves scientifically by photo-experiments the possibility of such reflected images in the human eye.

1966   May 31st: Pope Paul VI sends a Golden Rose to the shrine of Our Lady of Guadalupe.

1975   Translation of the sacred image from the old basilica, in danger of subsidence, to a new modern temple nearby.

1979   January: Pope John Paul II visits the shrine of Our Lady of Guadalupe, the first pontiff in history to do so.

1979   May: the sacred image is subjected to infra-red radiation examination by two American scientists. Their subsequent report confirms the supernatural nature of the portrait.

1981   450th anniversary of the apparitions: celebrations throughout Mexico.

BIBLIOGRAPHY

The following modern volumes are of particular importance and have been selected from the enormous bibliography on Guadalupe.

Behrens, Helen, *America's Treasure, The Virgin of Guadalupe,* printed in Mexico: Apartado 26732, Mexico 14 D.F., 1964. Also *The Lady and the Serpent,* 1966, by the above publishers.

Burland, C. A., *Art and Life in Ancient Mexico,* Oxford, 1947.

Demarest, Donald and Taylor, Coley, *The Dark Virgin, The Book of Our Lady of Guadalupe.* A documentary anthology. Academy Guild Press, 1959.

Dyal, Paul, *Empress of America,* a pilgrimage brochure, Auto Viajes Internacionales, 1959.

Keyes, Frances Parkinson, *The Grace of Guadalupe,* New York, 1941.

Lee, Reverend George, *Our Lady of Guadalupe,* published in 1896.

Rahm, Reverend Harold, *Am I not here?* A.M.I. Press, Washington N.J., 1963.

Taylor, Coley, *Our Lady of the Americas, Columbia,* December 1958.

Trappist Abbey Monks, *Our Lady of Guadalupe: the Hope of America,* Lafayette, Oregon.

Vaillant, G. C., *Aztecs of Mexico,* Pelican Books, 1965.

Wahlig, Dr. Charles, *A Handbook on Guadalupe* 1974, and *Juan Diego,* 1972, both books published by the Franciscan Marytown Press.

White, Jon Manchip, *Cortes and the downfall of the Aztec Empire,* Hamilton, 1971.

GENERAL INDEX